IT CAME TO PASS
In The San Juan Islands

by
Roderic Marble Olzendam
and
Gordon Keith

Binford & Mort
Thomas Binford, Publisher

2536 S.E. Eleventh • Portland, Oregon 97202

FOREWORD

In the San Juan Islands the Episcopal Church numbers some 300 members. As Episcopalians we know that we cannot make a total success of our lives without the help of God. Jesus Christ is the basis of our faith as he is revealed through the Holy Scriptures and in the lives of people.

Many are aware of a Power in this Universe which is instantly available to every man, woman and child. This Power, man calls God.

Since 1885 people have come from far and near, in good times and bad, to seek God in this lovely little chapel on the rocks by the sea. In a few fleeting years man will celebrate 100 years of worship in Emmanuel Church on the Isle of Orcas, where the power of God working through the people of this church—as in other churches of the Lord—has done wondrous things.

How does one acquire this power from God?

Let us imagine a Universal broadcasting network called 'C-O-S-M-O-S' from which programs are sent throughout the firmament twenty-four hours a day. This unique station, located in infinite space, boasts the Holy Spirit of God as its anchorman. One way is to sit quietly relaxed, with a clear and open mind and say aloud the following prayer:

"O God of peace, who has taught us that in returning and rest we shall be saved, in quietness and in confidence shall be our strength; by the might of Thy Spirit lift us, we pray thee to Thy presence, where we may be still and know that Thou art God."

(From 'The Book of Common Prayer')

Now, continue to sit quietly, expectantly, and eventually you will hear the Holy Spirit on your own personal wave length. God is calling. Listen, and do not tune Him out until His complete message has reached your inner consciousness.

Since the beginning of time, mankind has, through prayer and meditation, tuned in on this Universal network to listen patiently for the word of God.

Although this book purports to be an informal history of the Episcopal Church in the San Juan Islands, it also contains interesting Christian memorabilia, both serious and humorous. Hopefully, you will enjoy its contents.

—Roderic Marble Olzendam

PREFACE

Before undertaking the writing of this book, the authors determined that a treatise on church history and those who make this sacred institution function, need not be stuffy. Quite the contrary, because the combined efforts, physical and spiritual, of those who have contributed to the building and support of these island churches have made this book a joy to write and, hopefully, interesting to read.

It should be noted that this volume focuses on the early history of the Episcopal Church in the San Juan Islands. Namely: Emmanuel on Orcas Island, St. David's on San Juan Island and Grace Church on Lopez Island. A brief summary of the efforts to establish Episcopal services on Shaw (St. Thomas), Waldron and Stuart islands is also included.

As all Episcopalians are well aware, the basic premise of the Episcopal faith, as with many other denominations, is to bring man to God, through His son, Jesus Christ as set forth in the Ten Commandments and the Sermon on the Mount. "Seek ye first the kingdom of God, and His righteousness; and all these things shall be added unto you." Matthew 6:33.

It is the hope of the authors that a book such as this may in some small way stimulate a desire in those who belong to no congregation, to attend a church of their choice, for such an affiliation can prove a spiritually fulfilling experience.

At this point it seems apropos to say that the word 'man' as used within the context of these pages refers to 'any human being regardless of sex or age; a member of the human race; Homo sapiens'. (From the American Heritage Dictionary.)

—The Authors
Orcas Island, Wa.

CONTENTS

ACKNOWLEDGMENTS

The authors are indebted to Dave Richardson, author of 'Pig War Islands,' for the generous use of his resource material relative to the early history of the San Juans; and to John Omwake for permission to reprint his article, 'The Bowdlerization of a Literary Treasure,' which first appeared in the *Times-News Weekender*, and to the Rev. George W. Wickersham, II, for permission to reprint 'The Dignity of Choice' from *The Living Church*.

Our thanks also to Father Johnson West, Vicar of Eastsound's Emmanuel Church, for his helpful suggestions and research on certain church history; and to Mary Boberg, our secretary, for her patience and efficiency.

A special thanks to the following denominations for filling out the authors' statistical questionnaire relative to church attendance in the San Juan Islands: St. Francis Parish, Friday Harbor; Emmanuel Church, Eastsound; St. David's Church, Friday Harbor; Friday Harbor United Presbyterian Church; the Christian Science Society, Friday Harbor; Church of Latter Day Saints, Friday Harbor; Friday Harbor Seventh Day Adventist Church and the Orcas Island Community Church.

Chapter One

Emmanuel Church, Orcas Island, During the Early Years

In the early eighteen hundreds Orcas Island, located in the upper, Northwest corner of Washington State, was a bustling farm community, thanks to its rich, virgin soil. A number of orchards which had been planted by earlier residents were producing an excellent quality of fruit. But by 1890 much of the island's government land had already been homesteaded.

The first census of San Juan County, taken in 1870, shows the population to be 554. By 1880, five years before Emmanuel Episcopal Church was erected, the population of the county was 948. By 1890 it had practically doubled with a total of 2,072 persons living in the county. Orcas Island's share of that total population for the years 1900 and 1910 was 833 and 1119 respectively as compared with today's population (1978) which is approximately 2,000.

In 1883, Sidney R.S. Gray, a recent transplant from England by way of Canada came to Orcas Island for the express purpose of establishing an Episcopal Church on this 57-square-mile island, largest by one square mile of all the others in this 172-island archipelago.

Bewhiskered, redheaded and ambitious, and in his early forties, Sidney Gray, according to those who knew him, would have faired better as a real estate agent, rather than a man of the cloth.

Gray's wife, Alma, who arrived on Orcas Island sometime after her husband, was a lady of refinement who graciously accepted her position as a rector's wife in the little Village of

Eastsound. No one knew until after the Grays had moved from the island that Mrs. Gray was the daughter of the then reigning Duke of Mecklenburg-Schwerin. This titled lady had met her husband-to-be in England where they had fallen deeply in love with each other. She had married Sidney Gray without parental consent and was thereafter disavowed by her family. Nor did Gray fair much better with his own parents, for they were angered at their son for marrying a "foreigner".

At the time of Sidney Gray's arrival on Orcas Island he had not yet been ordained into the ministry, but this did not stop him from heading an Episcopal movement as lay missionary.

James Francis Tulloch, who came to Orcas Island in 1875 and remained until 1910, tells in his 100-year-old diary, which he wrote at the request of his daughter, Isabel, about his first meeting with S.R.S. Gray:

"We had a visit from three gentlemen who introduced themselves as Dr. Nevins, the Episcopal Minister of Olympia, Dean Watson of St. Mark's Church of Seattle and S.R.S. Gray, a landscape painter from Detroit who was taking Holy Orders.

"They came to me, they said, because I was supposed to be the leading man on the island as they wanted me to help them. I listened to their taffy and told them there must be some mistake, for not only did I not claim to be a leading man, I did not belong to their church and could not subscribe to their doctrines. They said it made no difference, that their church was very liberal on all questions of personal opinion. That I was a man of good moral standing and one who was very anxious to bring in decent families, that I knew that a church established would be the best of all drawing cards. I admitted this readily and they stayed with us that night. The outcome was that I became their church treasurer and a member of the vestry and subscribed $25 per year towards Mr. Gray's stipend, or salary which I afterword increased to $35 on condition that Gray should give my children lessons in Latin, etc.

"As I had much to do with Mr. Gray in after life, I wish to say a few words here as to what manner of man he was. S.R.S. Gray was a young Englishman of good family and fairly well educated, who lived by his wits in many lands. He was an extremely likeable and gentlemanly fellow who could talk a bird off a bush. He was a keen businessman, but one who in financial matters was absolutely unscrupulous who evidently took up the church calling as an easy and secure living. His great mistake was in not becoming a real estate agent.

"The church, when built in 1885, was duly consecrated as Emmanuel Episcopal Church and aided considerably in bringing in families. But I was continually in hot water for Gray would not account to me for collections made if he could possibly avoid it. His recklessness and extravagance would have swamped us if I had not constantly opposed him. He took my opposition always in good part, but his wife fairly detested me.

"Gray induced us of the vestry to go on a joint note for $500 for the material for an addition to the church, pledging us that he would get the amount long before it would be due. When the time arrived and he had not made good I took my part of it and asked the others to join me and pay it off. Gray interferred and told them to just give a new note in its place and he'd soon get it from his church friends.

"Also, while they were at it, just make it for $750 as a little extra money would sure come in handy. This angered me and I told him that I stood ready to pay my share of the $500, but if they gave a new note I certainly would not go on it. Nor would I pay one cent when it came due and I handed in my resignation as treasurer.

"Hambly said let him go, we can get along without him, but Gray said, 'By no means; I'd rather have any other dozen men down on me than Tulloch'.

"So I kept off the note and after Gray left (the island) they had it all to pay."

An early-day photograph of Emmanuel Church, located in Eastsound Village on Orcas Island in the San Juans. Built in 1885, this quaint little mission has had much loving care by its parishioners. In 1950 a parish hall was added and in 1967 a bell and belfry were donated by Roderic and Dorothy Olzendam.

James Tulloch goes on to tell about another incident he experienced with The Rev. Gray:

"I remember one evening I went up to pay $5 I owed at the store and Dean Watson of Seattle being there and holding services, I went into the church and when they took up the inevitable collection I put in a nickel as I supposed, knowing that I had one in my pocket. Remembering about the $5 I found it was gone and the nickel was still there. After services I mentioned it to Gray. He laughed and said he guessed the church was that much ahead. After he looked and found it (five dollar gold piece) he asked Dean Watson what he would do and

Temporary chancel, Emmanuel Episcopal Church, 1887, Eastsound, Washington Territory. Rev. S.R.S. Gray, Minister.

the Dean told us of one of his parishoners who had made a mistake and dropped in a marked silver dollar (into the collection plate) that was an heirloom in his family. The man wanted to give another dollar in exchange, but the Dean told him that a $20 gold piece would be about the same size and that they would settle it on that basis, which they did.

"I said, all right Mr. Gray, you keep my $5 gold piece and I'll just deduct it from your stipend." That didn't seem to please him and in fact it seemed to take all the fun out of the joke.

"Another time Gray came to see me late at night to endorse a note for him for several hundred dollars, which I positively refused to do. He was very angry about it, but I never would endorse anyone's note and certainly not his, for he never paid anything. He brought in a lot of so-called Missionary goods from his church in the East and proceeded to make himself solid by distributing them among his church members. I indignantly refused them and told him I was not a pauper and that I paid for all that my family wore. That the whole thing was a fraud as the members of his church were not subjects of charity, but were all fairly well off. I told him I would not touch the stuff with a ten foot pole. He said 'That's just some of your Scotch pride again'. But tho I had more to do with Gray than anyone else on the island, I had never lost a cent by him and when he left behind him a great many checks with no funds to meet them, he owed me nothing.

"With all his misdoings he was a man of so much personal magnetism and so much intelligence that it was impossible not to like him."

The early background of Emmanuel Church, like many rural churches, was fraught with problems of one sort or another. Lulu Kimple, who came to Orcas Island in 1883, points up one such problem in an article she wrote for the *San Juan Islander* newspaper:

"A man whose name I do not remember bargained for a lot from Charles Shattuck (a former Fraser River gold miner who homesteaded on Orcas Island circa 1860) on which to put up a saloon.

"I don't think the 'Women's Christian Temperance Union' was organized on the island until later, but the church women got together and protested so strongly that the man was scared and gave up his project, after having cleared the lot and put in the foundation for the building. My mother was a leader in this fight and I remember the excitement very well.

"Other leaders in the fight to eliminate a saloon on Eastsound's main street were messdames, Michael Donahue, John Madison, John Fry and Louisa Wright.

"That was the first and last attempt to start a saloon on the island."

Shortly after the Episcopal trio met with James Tulloch in 1883 to discuss plans for establishing an Episcopal Church on Orcas Island, Sidney Gray began to organize an Episcopal congregation. Not only did the ambitious Gray design Eastsound's Emmanuel Church, which he patterned after small village churches he had seen in England, but his grandiose plans included a replica of a model English village which was destined to become Orcas Island's first subdivision, and which he named Village de Haro.

The de Haro plat included the Madrona Point area of Eastsound and called for the establishment of commercial businesses, a rectory, a de Haro school for boys and St. Agnes school for girls.

Most islanders had grave doubts that Gray's plans for erecting a model English village on the island were feasible. Their primary concern was where the funds for such an enterprising venture would come from. However, if Elder Gray, as he was called, had any such doubts he kept them strictly to himself, for he was a positive thinker and a first rate motivator.

When Gray realized the success E.V. Von Gohren was having with his apple orchard, he was quick to see the financial potential for a commercial fruit industry on Orcas Island. While Von Gohren had actually pioneered the apple industry on the island, it was The Rev. S.R.S. Gray who interested outside capital in investing in the orchard business. As a result, two huge apple orchards were begun. Namely, the Charles Setzer homestead of 160 acres (Fruit Farm) and presently owned by the Y.M.C.A. The other was the former R.H. Anthony property just east of Eastsound.

Outside capital for the new business venture came from J.D. Lowman, Bernard Pelly (Pelly & Lowman), W.A. Peters, John Powell, Don Baxter and John W. Pratt.

During the peak season Eastsound shipped as many as 160,000 boxes of apples annually. Other areas, such as Olga, West Sound and Deer Harbor were also busy shipping fruit and at one time seven steamboats made regular trips between Orcas Island, Bellingham, Seattle and Port Townsend.

Recounting the Rev. Sidney Gray's numerous religious and business activities during those early years leaves no doubt that he was the community's leading light. Aside from designing Emmanuel Church, the plans for which included a vested choir such as he had known in England*, and platting Village de Haro, Gray's religious schedule included two Sunday services and a Wednesday evening prayer meeting and choir practice, plus calling on his parishoners.

His extra curricular activities consisted of selling lots in Village de Haro, being a notary, building a rectory and inducing outside investors to furnish funds for Orcas Island's growing fruit industry, which Gray played a major part in organizing. He was also superintendent of two or three local corporations and helped found the "Orcas Island Fruit Co.", "Orcas Island Canning & Buying Co.", as well as "Orcas Island Hop Co." His de Haro school for boys and St. Agnes school for girls reached the stage where letterheads for the project were in the mail requesting funds for the two schools, which, alas, like a number of Gray's other business ventures failed to materialize.

Had it not been that Baring Bros., International Bankers of London, closed their doors for business in 1891, The Rev. Sidney Gray might well have realized his dream of an English style village on Orcas Island. However, when the cabled news reached the Puget Sound area every banking house closed its doors.

Wrote Ben E. Harrison, who came to Orcas Island in 1890: "What a crash! How faired the rector? Of course he went broke. I saw him sitting in his study with his elbows on his desk and his head in his hands. I never saw more abject misery, and Eastsound never got back its promise of 1890."

According to another Orcas Islander, M.L. Kimple, who came to the area in 1883, Sidney Gray believed that everybody on Orcas Island stood to strike it rich by growing fruit commercially. Not so. When Eastern Washington apple orchards began to compete for the apple market (it was alleged that Orcas apples were inferior in size and color to Eastern Washington apples) this sounded the death knell for the island's commercial fruit industry.

The crash of 1891 and the loss of Orcas Island's apple market literally marked the downfall of The Rev. Sidney R.S. Gray's complex community plans. The decline of the island's prosperity and population shortly after the crash had a great deal to do with the decrease in the Episcopal congregation. People began to move from Orcas Island and church attendance, which had previously seen people standing for each service, dropped drastically. The depression lasted three years. Rev. Gray lost everything in the crash. He was not only despondent over his own losses, but those of his friends and associates who had invested in the orchard business at his suggestion. In 1893 Gray resigned as minister of Emmanuel Church and moved to Illinois where he later resumed his duties in another Episcopal church.

On October 9, 1893 members of the vestry drafted the following resolution on behalf of The Rev. Sidney Gray:

Emmanuel Parish
Eastsound, San Juan County
Washington, Oct. 9, 1893

At a meeting of the vestry of the church held this evening the following resolution was made and carried unanimously:

Resolved that we regret to learn that circumstances compel our rector (The Rev. S.R.S. Gray) to sever his connection with the parish, furthermore, we take this opportunity to testify to Mr. Gray's timely work for eight years amongst us, not only in church work but also in furthering all interests in this community. Resolved that a copy of this resolution be sent to Mr. Gray with our best wishes for his future welfare.

(signed) Norman Dixon; M.S. Donahue; Eph Langell;
William Hambly; C.H. Williams, Sec.

* While the little church boasted a large choir during The Rev. S.R.S. Gray's pastorate, it never obtained the vestments.

Chapter Two

The Reverend 'Sid' Gray

Excerpts from the letters of Richard H. Geoghegan to Flora Sutherland, dated 1892-1900 relating to Emmanuel Church and The Rev. Sidney R.S. Gray.

(NOTE: Richard H. Geoghegan came to Orcas Island in 1891. A gifted linguist, he and Dr. Zamenenhoff originated the Esperanto language. It was Richard Geoghegan who wrote the first Esperanto dictionary.

After leaving Orcas Island Geoghegan went to Alaska where he resided for over 40 years. A one-time British vice-consul in Seattle and Tacoma, Geoghegan was for many years an interpreter in the United States courts of Alaska.

In 1945 the Department of the Interior announced publication of an Aleut dictionary by Richard Geoghegan. Pronounced by the department as "one of the world's learned philologists" he was at the time of his death in 1944, just completing a translation from Russian of an Aleut-Russian dictionary dated 1834. Geoghegan substituted an alphabet of 18 English letters to represent all the sounds in the Aleut tongue. He was credited with a thorough knowledge of 200 languages and dialects.)

Eastsound, April 26, 1893

Dear Flora:

. . .Today the Odd Fellows and Rebekahs are celebrating their anniversary. They are to attend divine service in all their gorgeous apparel and afterwards have a dance & supper.

Week before the bishop of Spokane was here and I **did** actually arise somewhere about 6 to go down to see him. He was kind enough to pay us the compliment of saying that such a pious family was an ornament to the township. Very kind of him, wasn't it? But it **must** have struck him as peculiar that the congregation was mostly all composed of one family. He had a confirmation Friday and Hetty and Helen Robb were initiated.

Last Sunday evening we actually had an amusing sermon from Sid (The Rev. S.R.S. Gray) for a change. He read us an excerpt about some youth who was a 'sorry scrub', from 'Pilgrim's Progress' and the audience snickered out loud. I expect if the Sutherland family had been there as well as our own pious lot there would have been quite a disturbance.

Eastsound, May 18, 1893
Dear Flora:

. . .This evening there is a 'Poverty Social' in the school house; it is needless to add that it is in aid of the church debt. Eastsound will be a dull hole indeed if its church debt ever gets paid up. The most enthusiastic citizens can hardly claim that the social whirl is particularly dizzying at any time in their city, but any semi-occasional spasm of excitement that does pass over the place (Eastsound) may usually be traced to the church debt as its starting point. Programs of this nature have been adorning the public edifices for the past week, and Merce has made up a killing costume out of gunny-sacks with fixings of salt bags. One boot and one shoe—the latter tied up with string and the former provided with patent hygenic ventilation around the toes—together with one white sock, and one red sock, a belt of sackcloth fastened with a brace of skewers, and a fossil headgear that may have enhanced the charms of some of Noah's spouses, complete the outfit.

John is rigged out in a pair of over-all pants and a coat burst open at every seam. He has been diligently occupied all afternoon in tearing holes in the pants and then patching them up in a most artistic fashion with shreds of old rope. There are to be prizes given to the maiden and youth who are judged to be attired in the most elegant raiment.

Yu air axed tu a povurty soshul what us foax of saint agnes guild is gojnter giv in the skule hous east sound thursdy May 18th 1893. Phun will begin at 9 oklock.

Rools an regilashuns

Chap. 1. Every wuman what kums must ware a kaliker dress an apurn or sumthin ekerly aproperit.

Chap. 2. Every man what kems must wear a flanil shurt.

Chap. 111. People what doant du what this sez will be tackzed ten sents extra.

These ruls must an shall b obade,

The hul soshul komitty will interdoos straingers an look after the bashful fellers.

Vittles will be dispensed doorin evnin. Dafee will b five sents. It will cost yew 10 sents tu git in. Doant go doodin yerself up bfor yew kum. Their will be resitaishuns an tabloze.

. . .Sunday before last there was no service; which was quite an event. Our man of God had gone to Tacoma to see the Bishop. Your respected mama and ours held a service for the young, but as the snows of over a quarter of a century are already bleaching my locks I didn't consider that it was my duty to attend. Last Sunday 'Sid' sent me a note asking me to read the evening service for him as he had a cold. I declined with thanks & he remarked to me before service; 'If I beckon to you, you can come up & read the lessons.' However, he didn't. so I was spared that pleasure.

Eastsound 4 June 1893
Dear Flora:
 'Sid' only returned this morning.
This time, to make up, he has brought another parson home

with him; so we shall have quite a grand service tomorrow. . . .
There is a rumor that Sid and family are going east, but I don't
know whether it is a fact. If he does I s'pose we must all turn
Methodists and swear off dancing and our numerous frivolities.
There was quite an exciting sermon at the heretical level last
week. It was stated as an example of the awful depravity of our
city, that a parson 'not a thousand miles off' had actually
announced **from the pulpit**(!) that a certain meeting of Odd
Fellows would be followed by a dance.

Where must the flock be getting to, when the pastor hath so
fallen from grace as to make such an announcement?

Eastsound, June 14, 1893
Dear Flora:
. . .The Methodists are going to give an ice-cream social on the
23rd in the hall, and those who worship other gods are conse-
quently much excited and hope to get off a strawberry banquet
before that date.

. . .The parson we had Sunday before last was a caution to
snakes, very ancient and spoke as if he was going to sleep all the
time, and the sermon was a frightful length.

. . .I suppose 'Pap' has shown you the note I wrote him for 'Sid'
on Monday, in which our venerated pastor saith that he guesses
he won't be able to visit Lopez till next month and is then going
to stay some days, if Pap can put him up. Sid is going away next
Monday again and Fred is going with him to Tacoma Wednesday. . .

Eastsound June 26, 1893
Dear Flora:
Yesterday eve., being the Sabbath—'Sunday'. I mean—and
our revered pastor having, as hath been the custom of late, left
his flock to chew the pastures of spiritual refreshing unattended
by his watchful care. . . .

Eastsound, December 10, 1893
Dear Flora:

. . . .The Guild is making valient efforts towards getting up a Christmas-tree for the Sunday school. I wrote a letter for them to Seattle, in which they put forth convincing arguments that Emmanuel Church possesses the banner S.S. of the state, and deserves at least a carload of elegant presents and adornments for its tree.

Friday Mr. Hambly brought round a document stating that our late lamented pastor had lived a righteous, sober and godly life during his residence amongst us, and was in all respects a worthy candidate for the position of a full-blown priest and Levite. The names of Messrs. Dixon, Hambly, Williams, Ed King, Willard K., and R.H.G. were written at the bottom in pencil & they were requested to fill out in ink. Of course I gladly added my testimony to poor Sid's excellent character. Mr. H (Hambly) showed me a long letter he had had from him. It was mostly about his new church, which he says is not up to very much. There has never been a resident parson there before. He ends up by asking Mamie to write to him, but sends no love or kisses for Flora or others; so I spose he must have found a new bevy of best-girls; Such is the consistency of man--.

The man of God preached two sermons last Sund. each three quarters of an hour; this is to make up for Christmas. He says he can't come then, they are going to have a big spree on Shaw (Island) and he must needs stay and see it. The Guild made $19.00 out of their social and by making raiment for Hammond; they have expended the vast sum of $5.00 on presents. . .I forgot to say that our beloved Sid said in his letter that he would hustle to have a box sent us from the east. We shan't do so badly if our heart-rending appeal to the Seattleites is answered too. . .Nin has just had a letter to say they have turned a deaf ear to our entreaties.

I fear it is too late for us to get anything in time now. Christmastide will be for us a season of sackcloth and ashes. No church, no tree, no Sidney, perhaps no dance. . . .

Eastsound, December 28, 1893
Dear Flo:

. . . .Haven't been to church since you departed. The Rev. er--er makes me tired; so we've turned atheist till such time as 'another takes his place'. Rev. Dixon was over Sunday and treated the citizens to an hour's twaddle; glad I had the sense not to go. The Sunday scholars recited and had their prizes given them. The Mater was much scandalized by the Dittimore maiden, who packed a doll with her into the house of the Lord, and had the audacity to use it in acting a bye-low song which she sang. Everyone thought it was charming except our Ma, who wants to write to the bishop about it.

. . . .There was a morning service Monday, but no tree. The Seattle box containing nothing but books & they were even kind enough to let us know we sent them 75c too little. After the guild sending them $10.00 to help out for the presents, you'd have thought they might have knocked off the six bits without doing any serious damage to their business interests. The box Sid promised did not come along. . . .

Old man Nielson from Doe Bay has been after me about some papers of his he says Sid has got; so I'll have to write to the 'dear departed one' soon.

Eastsound, January 17, 1894
Dear Flo:

. . . .I had a long letter from Sid last week. He wants Flora and his other best-girls to write to him. He didn't say very much; mostly a history of his services. He has a morning performance at 7:30: I wonder how he managest to get up in time. . . He hopes we all do what we can to keep up the services of God's house, and that we had a good time at Christmas.

Dear Flo,   Eastsound, January 17, 1894
. . . .The Rev. Dyer was spilt out of his boat the other day, but a bible he had in his pocket floated him. He has been regretting that it was not in his valise, as that went to the bottom.

My dear friend,   Eastsound, Jan. 10, 1894

. . . .Donkey Dickson (The Rev. John William Dickson from Shaw Island who used to bring his horse or donkey tied to a raft behind his rowboat when he came to Orcas Island to preach at Emmanuel Church) told the populace in his Sunday sermon that Sid had been made a priest, so I guess he is now happy, and reconciled to leaving Eastsound and his dear girls. I can't imagine why he doesn't write to us.

My Dear Flo: Tacoma, July 3, 1896

. . . .Glad to know you are enjoying yourself so well. . . . The Bishop is to leave Thursday for the islands and I believe intends taking the Eastsound choir around with him to the divers places he is going to favor with his presence. So if you want to go around with them and hear his latest puns and help demolish the ice cream, you must get Dickson to let you warble in the choir for the time being. . .

Chapter Three

Two Years Go By Before
Emmanuel Church has a Full Time Vicar

As far as can be determined the first church registry ends with the resignation of the Rev. Sidney R.S. Gray. In an entry dated October 6, 1893 and certified by John Henry Forest Ball, Priest, there is a listing of 'furniture, books, ornaments, etc.', turned over to a committee consisting of Thomas Dixon and William Hambly.

Following the Rev. Gray's resignation in 1893 Emmanuel Church was without a regular minister for two years. Then in 1895 the Rev. John William Dickson took over as minister of the church.

It is interesting to note that in May of 1945 Harding Gow, whose recollections of Orcas Island date back to 1896 when he first came to Orcas, wrote about Emmanuel Church and the Rev. Dickson as follows:

"When I first knew Eastsound, the Episcopal Church was the center of many community activities and the rector was one of the most remarkable men I have known.

"Rev. John William Dickson succeeded the now, almost legendary Sidney R.S. Gray as rector in 1895 and continued in that capacity until 1904.

"He conducted services and preached a sermon in Emmanuel Church every Sunday morning, then mounted his faithful horse and rode the nine miles to Orcas, loaded his horse into the pot scow and rowed across to Shaw Island. There he beached the scow, mounted his horse and rode to the meeting place of his flock.

"After service and sermon he returned to Eastsound by the same route and preached a sermon in the evening. In addition to his parishoners, he ministered to the sick, looked after the finances of his parish and was a leader in all community, social activities.

"I think Rev. Mr. Dickson came the nearest to deserving the name of 'Saint' of any man I have ever met. His patience was infinite and his resignation and sense of humor are well illustrated by a story that was told of him:

"He had saved for a long time to buy a cow and at last he had the funds in hand and had started for the mainland to select the animal. The boat met with rough water and the reverend gentleman got seasick—and his false teeth followed his lunch overboard. Sick as he was he managed to muster up a wry smile and say: 'Well, there went my cow.' "

During the years The Reverend John William Dickson conducted services at Emmanuel Church in Eastsound Village, he also held services at West Sound, in the only other Episcopal Church on the island.

Following Dickson's departure from Orcas Island in 1904, Emmanuel Church suffered serious neglect in upkeep for a number of years.

In 1916, The Rev. Henry J. Purdue, former archdeacon from Spokane, succeeded The Rev. John William Dickson as pastor of both the Eastsound and West Sound Churches. The church register shows but few entries during The Rev. Henry Purdue's ministry.

Roger Purdue, son of The Rev. Henry Purdue, has this to say about his father's ministry at Emmanuel Church:

"When my father took over the duties of the church in 1916 there were only eight or ten and sometimes as few as three or four members who attended church services, but father held services just the same.

"On Christmas Eve, when my father always gave out presents around the church Christmas tree to the kids and some of the grownups, he would always have a packed house."

The following entries were made in the church register prior to The Rev. Purdue's move to Orcas Island. He often conducted church services during his summer vacations on the island.

"Aug. 2, 1914: Services were held by the venerable Henry J. Purdue, Archdeacon of Spokane, 61 were present. Offering, $7.71; 48 were present at evening services, offering, $2.21.

"Aug. 9: Morning prayer and sermon, 49 present, offering, $5.50. Evening prayer and sermon, 39 present, offering, $1.31.

"Aug. 16, Holy Communion and Sermon: 38 present, offering, $5.81. Total $22.54.

"This money was spent by the undersigned to Rt. Rev. F.W. Keator, D.D. to pay general diocesan apportion."

During its early years, West Sound's Episcopal Church which was built in 1895, enjoyed a sizeable congregation. However, with the drastic decline in Orcas Island's commercial fruit industry, people began to move from the island. Church attendance also declined to such an extent that the West Sound Church closed its doors. Then around 1924 a number of recalcitrant teenage boys, cruising the West Sound area in a Model 'T' Ford deliberately threw lighted matches into the dry grass in front of the little church, burning it to the ground. Roger Purdue, along with Nova Langell and other volunteer firemen helped extinguish the fire, but not before it had burned over a large section of the hillside.

When the Rev. Henry Purdue retired from the ministry after some fifteen years service with the church, future services were held sporadically over the next few years and were generally conducted by various visiting priests.

Around 1932 Mrs. Harding Gow and Miss Jessie Templin, unable to stand by and watch Emmanuel Church continue to deteriorate because of the elements and a lack of proper care, raised enough money to have the church shingled. They reasoned that the small mission at least might serve as a sort of shrine of the past.

Then, in September of 1942 The Rev. Oliver Drew Smith was appointed vicar of Emmanuel Church. The Reverend commuted from Mt. Vernon to Orcas Island and thereafter services were held every Sunday. Later, a Bishop's Committee was formed which consisted of Harding Gow, Senior Warden; William Perry, Clerk; Curtis Bailey, Walter Redford, John Sorenson; Mrs. Charles Sorenson and Jessie Templin.

Emmanuel's church ledger shows that under The Rev. Sidney R.S. Gray's administration the sermons were "vigorous and informative" and were conducted with "great solomnity and the music was good, too."

The church registry, which begins with the consecration of Emmanuel by The Right Reverend John Adams Paddock, missionary bishop of Washington on December 13, 1885, contains a list of 414 members.

According to Margaret (Maggie) Gaggs, who prepared an historic summary of Emmanuel Church's 75th Anniversary, the lettering in the church ledger could only have been done by Henry (Richard) Geoghegan, whose ability with a lettering pen was remarkable.

In another entry, this one undated, there were 221 members listed, while a third list includes 72 communicants. Although these lists are not dated, when compared with other entries in the ledger which bore dates, it is probably safe to assume that the membership figures quoted were during the middle, or later years, of The Rev. Sidney Gray's pastorate on Orcas Island.

Other early entries contain such quaint facts as the burial of Etta King who died April 29, 1887 and who was married as the register notes "8 mos., less 1 day. Quick decline."

The cause of death of the twenty-one-month-old child of Joseph Bull is written as "Fell in a tub of boiling water." Other causes of death show that Margaret Alice McBride died September 21, 1888, aged 15 months, of "nervous prostration" and that William Herschell Caldwell who died May 20, 1890 aged 64 was "worn out".

The first person to be buried in the then new Mt. Baker Cemetery was Grace Donahue, age 14, who died November 15, 1890 of "anemia".

First to be baptized in the new church were William, Ellen, Maryanne and Frederick Hambly. Others include Henry Thomas Cayou, August 8, 1886 and on the same date were the seven children of James and Marry Ann Tulloch. (The Tullochs later had two more children.) Alma Gray, wife of The Rev. Sidney Gray, appears in the register as sponsor of the seven Tulloch children. Also baptized was a group of five children belonging to Ephraim and Rose Langell.

The ledger shows that on October 3, 1886, Louisa Jane Cayou was baptized. The entry signed by The Rev. S.R.S. Gray, General Missionary, may indicate that Gray was consecrated as priest between that date and December 14, 1885 when he signed a record of baptism by Bishop Paddock of the Van Sant and Robb children as "Lay Missionary in charge".

Between the years, 1950 and '52, Emmanuel Church had another commuting vicar, The Rev. George Pratt who commuted between Abbotsford, British Columbia and Orcas Island. The Rev. Pratt's first service drew 13 communicants. He had recently given up a thriving parish in Stockton, California with some 1300 communicants, in order to be near his aging parents. It was during The Rev. Pratt's ministry that electricity was first installed in the Eastsound Episcopal Church.

Chapter Four

Father Johnson West Arrives on Orcas Island

On April 5, 1953, Father Johnson West conducted his first service at Emmanuel Church in the village of Eastsound. His second service was in August of that same year. Then, on February 7, 1954, Father West became vicar of Emmanuel Church. During this same period he also conducted services twice a month at Valley Church on San Juan Island. In 1955 services were moved to a vacant downtown store in Friday Harbor. From then on services were held weekly.

The first church services held by Father Johnson West on Lopez Island were held bi-monthly in the home of Mrs. Russell Knight. They were later moved to Valley Church on that island where they were held weekly.

It is interesting to note that a bit of friction arose among a few of the parishoners of Emmanuel Church because they deemed it unnecessary for Father West to travel to Lopez Island in order to re-establish church services, particularly when there was but one Episcopalian on the entire island.

"But the Bishop clarified the issue," Father West explained, "by pointing out to the parishoners that the purpose of the mission was to bring Christ into the lives of those who don't know Him. And that was reason enough for me to conduct services on Lopez Island. Thus it was that I went to Lopez."

In the late spring of 1955, Father Johnson West, determined to increase Episcopal worship in the San Juans, made a number of trips to Waldron Island to visit with some of the old timers. His express purpose for going was to arrange church services on

Father Johnson West, Vicar of Emmanuel Church on Orcas Island, reads from the Bible during "Seder," which he first introduced to members of Emmanuel Church in 1975. Says Father West: "I would like to point out that "Seder" is extremely important to all Christians when we realize that this Jewish religious celebration has been going on for some 4,000 years and represents the oldest continuing celebration known to man." *(Photo by Gordon Keith)*

that quaint little 4.5 square mile island with its 40, year-round residents.

A date was finally set for Waldron Island's first Episcopal service which was to be held in the schoolhouse. On the evening of the scheduled service, Galen Burghardt took a load of Orcas Island parishoners to Waldron in his power boat. However, when the expectant party arrived dockside, they were informed that the planned service had been suddenly cancelled. (Waldron Island has neither telephones, nor electricity.)

"We really never learned first hand the full story as to why the service had been cancelled so abruptly," said Father West. "However, it was strongly rumored that there had been some

sort of 'book-burning' a few days before by a group of Waldron-
ites who strongly opposed any religious activities on the island."

Father West points out that the burning of all religious and
philosophical books on the island was strictly heresay. But the
fact remains that for a number of years, there were no
Episcopal Church services on Waldron Island.

On Christmas day in 1955, Father Johnson West held his first
service in the Shaw Island schoolhouse with some thirty people
in attendance. However, this proved to be a one-time service for
there just weren't enough Episcopalians on the island at that
time who were ready for on-going church services.

While still in seminar and believing that God had called him
to serve in the military as a Chaplain, Father Johnson West requested permission to serve his country in that capacity. In 1955
the Bishop granted his request and in 1956 Father West was
commissioned an Air Force Chaplain. Although he had always
planned to return to Orcas Island, he hoped as Vicar of
Emmanuel Church, of the latter he couldn't be sure.

As things turned out, Father West's hopes were eventually
realized, but not until the summer of 1973, some 18 years later.

Chapter Five

Enter Father Glion Benson

When Father Johnson West returned to active duty as Chaplain in the Air Force, Father Glion Benson, who had been serving as vicar of St. James Episcopal Church in Sedro Woolley, was transferred to Emmanuel Church on Orcas Island as vicar. His duties were to serve the entire San Juans. A large order, area-wise, for it meant traveling from island to island by ferry boat. Ferry schedules being subject to a number of uncontrolable variables, namely, the weather, made inter-island trips very time consuming and somewhat uncertain. When the ferry was late, so were the services.

In 1957 the Daughters of the King, aware of Father Benson's need for adequate transportation, offered to give him $2000 with which to purchase a bus. However, Bishop Stephen Bayne of the Diocese of Olympia suggested that a boat would serve as a more practical means of island transportation.

Fortunately, Father Benson had had considerable experience with boats, having worked as an oiler and engineer on a number of merchant marine vessels on the East coast, following his discharge from the U.S. Navy after World War One. He was very knowledgeable about marine motors, including diesels, and was regarded as an expert in this field.

With the money received from the Daughters of the King Father Benson bought a 26-foot converted Navy diesel whaler which he christened the 'Royal Cross'. The boat made it possible for him to hold regular Sunday morning services on time at

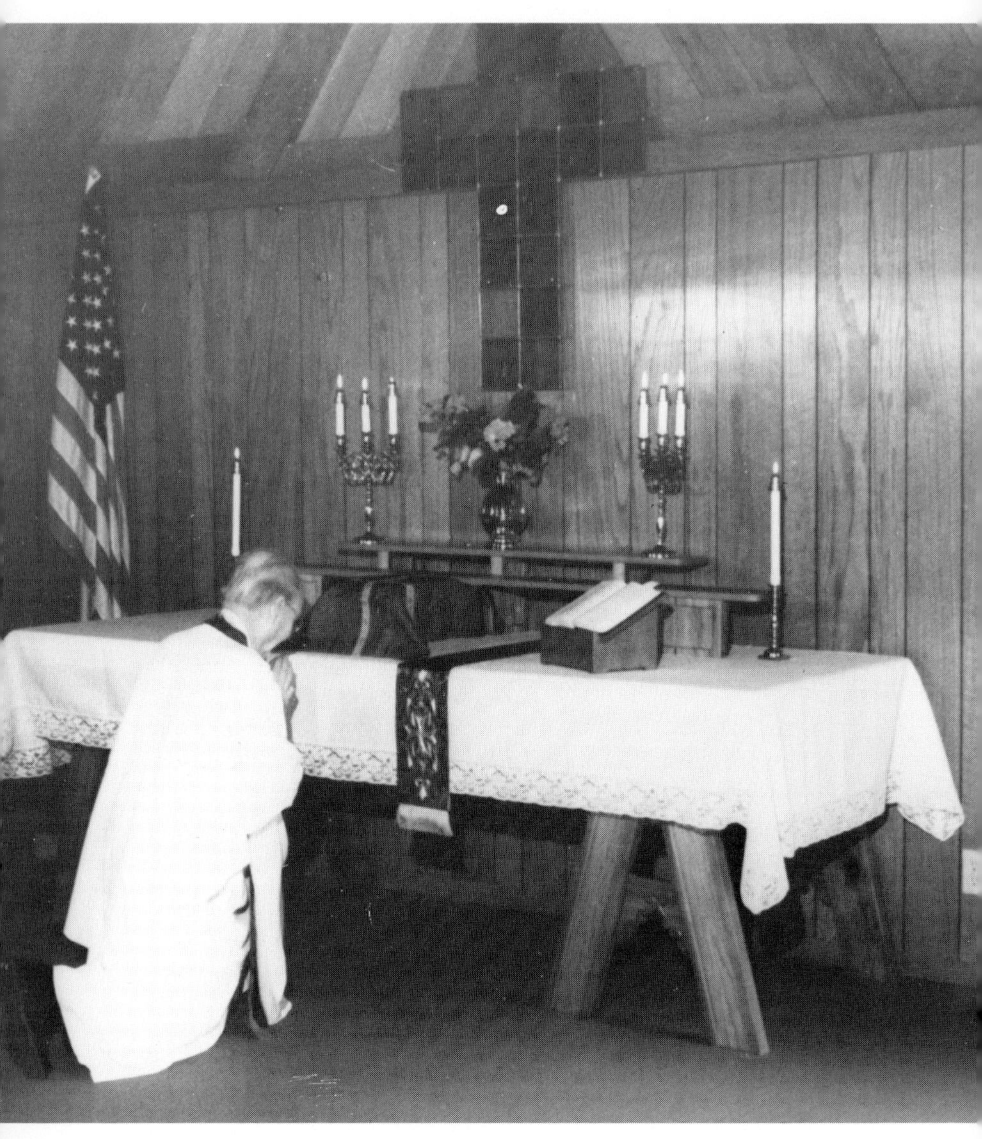

Father Glion Benson kneels before the altar in Grace Church on Lopez Island, 1970. The legs of the table were copied from da Vinci's "Last Supper."

Orcas, Lopez and San Juan Islands. It also afforded him an opportunity to visit parishoners living on some of the smaller islands, not accessible by ferry. It wasn't long before he became known affectionately by the press and islanders alike as the "Seagoing Vicar" of the San Juans.

Father Benson's schedule in those years was somewhat hectic in that he held services on Orcas Island at 8:00 a.m. and 10:00 a.m. after which he and his wife, Jean ("Mother" Benson to her many island friends) would pack their lunch and board the "Royal Cross" and head for Fisherman's Bay on Lopez Island where parishoners would take them by car to Center Church (Grace Church hadn't been built at that time) in time for the 2:30 p.m. service. After the service the Bensons would return to their boat and sail for Friday Harbor where they would conduct an 8:00 p.m. service. Services were then held in a vacant store on Spring Street.

That night they would sleep in a small room at the back of the store on a folding cot, which, according to "Mother" Benson, left a lot to be desired insofar as comfort went. In the morning Father Benson would visit various members of the parish. Then at 2:30 p.m. the Bensons would again board the "Royal Cross" and return to their home base on Orcas Island.

Father Benson's early morning ritual at Emmanuel Church was to light the oil furnace at the front of the church as well as the one in the parish hall. This was done by first setting fire to a piece of paper and then dropping it into the furnace. It was while lighting the parish hall furnace one morning in 1958 that Father Benson had his first heart attack. Unable to carry on with his church duties, his good friend Roderic Olzendam took over the services for the following three months while he was recuperating.

In 1966 Father Glion Benson was made Honorary Canon of St. Mark's Cathedral in Seattle, Washington. Bishop Stephen Bayne also granted him a lifetime appointment of Canon Missioner.

In 1968 Father Benson had another serious heart attack. It was then that "Mother" Benson insisted that he give up the "Royal Cross" and that same year Father Benson retired from the ministry. He did, however, continue conducting church services on Orcas and Lopez Islands to help Father Ted Leche, the San Juan Islands' new vicar. Father Benson continued in this capacity even after Father Johnson West returned to take over services at Emmanuel Church in 1974.

Blessed with a great sense of humor, Father Benson often referred to himself as "God's recycled altar boy". During an interview with a local reporter, when asked what his religious title was, he replied, tongue in cheek:

"I'm a Canon Missioner and make sure you spell Canon with one 'n'. 1 don't want anyone to get the idea I'm a big shot."

Over the years Father Glion Benson's knowledge of diesel engines has often stood him in good stead, such as the time a palatial yacht ran into engine trouble near the Orcas ferry landing.

The incident occurred early one Saturday morning when the vessel's owner found his boat dead in the water. A Canadian and a stranger to this particular area, the skipper needed someone experienced with diesel engines to get it running. Somebody suggested getting in touch with Glion Benson.

At the time Father Benson was enroute by car to Deer Harbor with the Reverend Walter McNeil who was making his annual visitation to Emmanuel Church.

An urgent call from the skipper of the stranded vessel to the ferry dock ticket office was relayed to Mother Benson at her home in Eastsound Village. She informed the caller, a parishioner, where Father Benson was headed and within minutes Father Benson and the Reverend McNeil were flagged down. The Reverend was then transferred to the parishoner's car, while Father Benson headed for the ferry landing where he was whisked by outboard to the stranded boat.

After spending considerable time checking over the ailing diesel engine (Father Benson was in street clothes at the time, hence, the vessel's skipper was unaware that the little old gentleman diagnosing the trouble was a man of the cloth) Father Benson pinpointed the problem as a damaged part, which the skipper ordered by telephone from the mainland and that afternoon the vessel was under way.

It wasn't until later, that Father Glion Benson learned that the boat he had worked on belonged to one of Canada's wealthiest men. Nor would it have made one iota of difference if he had known, for to Father Glion Benson all are the Lord's children and as such are entitled to his help, whether rich or poor.

While Emmanuel Church is one of the most photographed tourist attractions on Orcas Island, this quaint little mission didn't just happen. It should be pointed out that many of its parishoners over the years have contributed generously, both in time and money, toward its upkeep. But it was Father Benson and his affinity for the sea, who was instrumental in erecting a facsimile of a ship's flagpole (donated by the Henry Isaacson family of Deer Harbor) which stands majestically overlooking the placid waters of Eastsound Village.

One of Father Benson's great delights was flying his ship's signal flags during the summer tourist months. Visiting boaters anchored in the nearby waters were often surprised to see various coded messages flying from the flagpole of Emmanuel Church:

U. You are standing in danger (Rocky Coast).
RS. Is all well with you?
RV. Where are you bound?
BOM. We will not abandon you. (Regardless of condition.)

Although Father Benson was officially retired in 1968, he continued to assist with various church services and functions under Father Ted Leche, who had been appointed Vicar of the San Juan Islands in 1967. However, failing health forced Father Benson into complete retirement in 1974.

Father Glion Benson of Emmanuel Church with his happy altar boys. *(Photo by Willard Stone)*

As has been previously noted, Father Glion Benson was truly the Lord's "handyman". Although he passed away on April 21, 1976, after a lengthy illness, at the age of seventy, the church yards are a living testimony to both Father and "Mother" Benson's gardening talents. The beautiful greensward which encompasses the church on either side is set off with vari-colored flowers and a white picket fence. Each spring a living cross of white crocuses, first planted in the church grounds by the Bensons, comes to life in a breathtaking array of natural beauty. A silent reminder of "God's recycled altar boy", Father Glion Benson.

Chapter Six

Father Johnson West Returns to Emmanuel Church

In 1974, after an absence of 18 years, Father Johnson West returned to take over as Vicar of Emmanuel Church. That same year, during an interview for the local paper Father West told how he first came to know Orcas Island:

"When I first served with the U.S. Air Force I was stationed at Clover Field (renamed Ault Airfield). Every chance I got I'd fly to the San Juans and 'buzz' Orcas Island. Even then I knew that someday I'd be making my home on that island."

What Father West did not know at the time was, that when he finally moved to Orcas it would be as Vicar of Emmanuel Church.

Although his father, Samuel E. West, was an Episcopal clergyman and his brother was studying for the clergy, his own career in the ministry never entered Johnson West's mind. Prior to the war he had been an undergraduate in forestry and his interests were solely in the realm of forestry and nature.

Preceding his Army Air Force years in World War Two, which ran from 1942 until 1946, Johnson West received a BA degree in botanical sciences. After his discharge from the service in 1946 as Lt. Col., he continued his forestry studies at the University of Washington. However, this project came to an abrupt end one night when he was suddenly awakened from a sound sleep:

"I received a 'call' from the Lord one night in which He indicated in no uncertain terms that I ought to change my life plans. All I can say is that the 'call' came to me in the middle of the night waking me from a sound sleep. You might say that one of the wonders of God's working is that even though I did not feel in any way suited, or qualified to serve in the ministry, when God's 'call' came it did so not only with incentive, but with the assurance that I could do what the Lord required of me."

So certain was Johnson West that the Lord wanted him to serve in the ministry that he discontinued almost immediately, his forestry studies and returned to the University of Wichita to pick up some neglected liberal arts courses he had previously ignored in his past studies.

In 1948, Johnson West entered Seabury-Western Theology Seminar in Evanston, Illinois. Following graduation in May of 1951, he was ordained a Deacon and in 1952 he was ordained a priest at the Episcopal Cathedral in Seattle, Washington. His first assignment was Vicar of a church in Blaine, where he was responsible for all of Whatcom County. Then in 1953 Bishop Stephen Bayne assigned Father West to Emmanuel Church on Orcas Island, making him the first resident priest responsible for all of the San Juan Islands' Episcopal congregations.

Even though Father West left the San Juans to enter the military in 1956, his official and legal residence since then has always been, Orcas Island.

In 1968 during a year which he spent as a flying Army Air Force Chaplain, Lt. Col. Johnson West saw many soldiers turn to God when all else failed.

"It was not uncommon," Father West said, "for a soldier to come to me and say: 'I've tried everything else and haven't found any real meaning to life, so what the heck have you got to offer, Chaplain?'

"And this is exactly the way many people feel about religion today. They want to do everything themselves. They fail to realize the importance of guidance from the One who put us together. When we begin to follow the manufacturer's recommendations some amazing things begin to happen. When we begin to take God at His word we soon discover that it's not what we do, but what we let God do through us that makes the big difference in our lives.

"The trouble is that a great many of today's young adults have never even stopped to think whether or not there is actually a God. They are too busy living their lives and trying to work out their problems by themselves. It's true that most people will admit that the bible is worthwhile reading. But on the other hand, a vast majority have never even read one epistle from the Bible."

Father West points out what a person with little or no working knowledge of God's power, can do to receive divine guidance in his or her daily life.

"First, I am reminded of the lad in John 6:9 who had five barley loaves and two small fishes to offer Jesus that He might feed a multitude of five thousand. The lad simply offered what he had and God did the rest.

"The same thing applies to us as individuals. We offer what we have and it is fantastic what He will do with it. Not because of our capabilities, knowledge, or wisdom, but simply because of our willingness to let God work His wonders through us."

That Father Johnson West practices what he preaches is attested to by his following statement:

"I look for great things. I expect great things and I can accomplish great things; not because of me, as an individual, but because of what God can do and because of what I have seen Him do. To God, nothing is impossible."

Over the years Emmanuel Church (Mother Church of the San Juan Islands) has reached out to provide missionary leadership and support of other island congregations. In November of 1974, the same year Father Johnson West returned as vicar, Orcas Island's Emmanuel Church was formally admitted to the Diocese as an organized mission in conformance with the requirements of Canon Law.

Chapter Seven

Saint Agnes Guild

According to available records Emmanuel Church's St. Agnes Guild was organized around 1932. However, within a few years Guild attendance had dwindled to such a degree that meetings were discontinued and it wasn't until 1939, when a small body of women got together and revived St. Agnes Guild, that it became an active church organization.

A sampling of the first St. Agnes Guild activities which have been taken verbatim from the Guild ledger reads as follows:

Nov. 2, 1939. St. Agnes Guild met at the home of Jessie Templin. Mrs. Templin read a letter from Bishop Huston giving the Guild authority to take charge of the church property. After which, Mrs. Arney was elected president, Mrs. Storey, Vice President and Mrs. Templin, Sec-Treas.

$46.35 was subscribed toward the building of a new fence around the church property.

Nov. 11/39: Plans were discussed for a White Elephant Sale at Madrona Club House on Nov. 18th. Men who volunteered to work on the fence included: H.W. Gow, Dave Nicol, Karl Templin, Pat Langell, Fred Nicol, A. Kerchoff and others.

July 10/39: After minutes were read C. Smith gave a talk telling what was needed at the church.

Under the direction of the Guild's first President, Mrs. Tvete, plans were formulated to acquire the necessary land upon which to construct a parish hall. By 1940 St. Agnes Guild held its first major sale for the express purpose of raising money to repair the church and establish a parish hall building fund. Since then the St. Agnes Guild Sale has been an annual event and very successful these sales have been.

Further excerpts from the official St. Agnes Guild records show the following entries:

Jan. 7/1941: 11 members present. Total collections $474.91. Mrs. Gow moved that $5 be sent to Bishop Huston for British War Relief.

May 6/41: Mrs. Gow presented a bill for altar carpet for $136.66.

July 1/41: Mrs. Tarte in chair. 23 present. $3.45 collection.

Aug. 5/41: The Guild gratefully accepted Mr. Fred Meyer's offer to hold the Bazaar at his hotel building (Outlook Inn). A note of thanks to Mrs. Robert Moran for stained glass windows. A motion was made and carried that the church be painted as soon as possible. The chair presented a gift of $26.50, donor unknown, to be used for foreign relief, 31 members present. Collections $5.00.

Sept. 22/41: Mrs. Moran moved that we go ahead with the stained glass windows. Motion carried. It was decided to get the church history in some kind of shape to make a booklet.

Nov. 4/41: Books reported to be in bad shape. Mrs. Hawkins to work on them. It was decided to put a brass plate by the windows.

May 7/42: Meeting opened with a reading from the hymnal 'For Those In Peril On The Sea'. Present, 25. Collected $3.70.

Aug. 4/42: Guild met to decide how to spend funds raised at the Bazaar. It was moved and carried to buy two, $100 war bonds, interest bearing war bonds and one $37.50, 10-year bond. Secretary instructed to purchase same and arrange with San Juan County Bank to hold them in trust.

Sept. 1/42: Secretary reported that from Nov. 2, 1939 to Sept. 1, 1942, $2087.81 was received. Balance in the bank, $364.27. Mrs. Karl Templin made her report on the ordering of the sign for the outside of the church. It was moved to sell the old windows of the church. It was moved and seconded to send $50 to the Chaplain's Fund. Secretary placed the receipt for safe keeping of War Bonds in the safe at Templin's Store.

Oct. 6/1942: Mrs. Gow unanimously elected Pres. Mrs. L. Larson, V.P., Miss Templin, Sec. Treas., Mrs. Gow gave a talk on Chinese and Russian relief and it was decided to devote our work to these important war efforts.

Nov. 3. 1942: Guild met with Mrs. Moran, $30 was collected for China War Relief.

Some expenditures for 1942: Painting church $83.70, Insurance $7.20, Red Cross $25.00, Army and Navy Com. $85.00, Labor on yard and church $46.14, China War Relief $222.00, Russian War Relief $31.15 and to Russia $177.00.

Mar. 7, 1944, Easter Egg hunt on the church grounds on Easter.

June 1, 1944: Mrs. Gow opened the meeting with a touching prayer for 'Invasion Day'.

Aug. 5, 1944: It was moved and seconded to spend $150 as follows: $100 Greek Relief and $50 for China Relief.

Oct. 1944: It was moved and carried not to meet next week but to spend a day at home sewing for the Guild.

Nov. 14, 1944: Fifth Anniversary of the Guild's reorganization (1939). It was voted to send $5.50 to the Bishop to cover error made by his bookkeeper.

Mar. 6, 1945: Our assignment to the Diocesan Missions came up for discussion but on account of our low funds in the bank it was decided to let it rest for a while.

Apr. 3, 1945: Easter tea was held at the home of Mrs. Gow. 40 men were present. The prize went to Miss Templin.

Mar. 5, 1946: The Guild met at the home of Mrs. Carl Tvete with ten members present.

A suggestion was made that the vestry be consulted as to the purchase of new prayer books and hymnals and purchase was advised.

The next business was the discussion of the possibility of purchasing the 30 foot strip of land adjacent to the church property on the east, preparatory to the building of a Parish House and cottage for a clergyman. It was truly ventured that an active cause brings in interest and money, where passive support fails.

Barton Green was appointed as a proper person to approach May Gerrard with an offer of $600 for the 30-foot strip.

The plowing of the church yard had not been accomplished so further efforts were advised.

Adenda: The discussion of quarters for O.D. Smith and his wife was also taken up. The Guild moved that quarters should be provided and subsidized from our treasury beyond the church collection.

In 1946 Bishop Stephen Bayne, Jr., of the Diocese of Olympia approached Fred P. Meyer, owner of 26 acres of land in Eastsound, including 'Outlook Inn' as well as the property where the Parish Hall now sets, with an offer to purchase the property adjacent to the church. According to Peter Vincent, grandson of Fred Meyer, his grandfather refused to sell the property. However, he would donate the land to the church for the parish hall, but with one proviso:

"My Grandfather agreed to give the land to the church provided Bishop Stephen Bayne would agree to perform the wedding of my sister, Martha and her fiance, Donald Trekell, in a High Mass ceremony at Trinity Church in Seattle. The Bishop consented and they were married, after which Grandfather turned over the deed to the land to Emmanuel Church as he had agreed.

"My folks weren't at all churchy," Peter Vincent said, "but they wanted to put on a fabulous wedding for my sister, which they certainly did.

"The Reception was held at the Rainier Club for some 1200 guests. Fourth Avenue was blocked off at 5 p.m. and all cars came across Fourth Avenue and turned left into the Rainier Club. What a traffic jam that was, but my Grandfather was a happy man."

One picture is worth a thousand words. *(Photo by Gordon Keith)*

Emmanuel Church's St. Agnes Guild Sale draws literally hundreds of enthusiastic shoppers, not only from Orcas Island and neighboring islands, but from the mainland as well. *(Photo by Gordon Keith)*

With the St. Agnes Guild's $5000 contribution, along with a number of generous gifts from interested donors and a loan from the Diocese of Olympia, the Bishop's Committee was able to order the construction of parish hall, the cost of which was in the neighborhood of $15,000.

At this point, however, all was not well with some members of the church for there were those who were not in accord with the building plans which called for attaching the parish hall onto the church.

Mrs. Harding Gow felt that the little church which the Rev. S.R.S. Gray had designed after an old English Church he had attended in England was architecturally perfect and she did not want its Gothic lines spoiled by adding the parish hall to it.

It is interesting to note that the Langells, who were active members of Emmanuel Church until 1948, when the parish hall was built, discontinued their membership as did Miss Templin. Their reason being that they were very much opposed to attaching the parish hall to the church proper. They felt strongly that by so doing the Gothic lines of the church had been destroyed.

Only once after the parish hall had been constructed did Wesley Langell enter the building and then only to buy a pair of trousers during the Guild's annual sale.

In early 1946 Guild records show that St. Agnes Guild held its regular meeting at the home of Mrs. Horace Dana in Olga, with 24 in attendance. President Mrs. Curtis Bailey presided.

The church yard, which had been plowed, but not furrowed, was discussed. A yard cleanup picnic was suggested and approved. June 29th was set for the meeting of the church. . . . It was planned to invite certain 'broad, able bodied men who would be willing to work two hours on the yard'. In return the Guild would furnish them with a fried chicken picnic supper at six o'clock.

Mrs. Barton Green and Mrs. C.R. Wright were appointed committee in charge. "A suggestion was made by our president that we offer to the Roman Catholics the use of our church whenever it did not interfere with our own services."

The following is taken from the minutes of the August 25, 1946 meeting of the Bishop's Committee of Emmanuel Church:

Mrs. Nova Langell, Chairman, and Mrs. Charles Bliss, Secretary, being unavoidably absent, Curtis Bailey was asked to act as Secretary pro tem to write the minutes. Mr. John Sorenson, a newcomer on the Committee was also welcomed into the fold.

The Committee expressed its gratification at the presence of Bishop Huston which was due to the first Confirmation Service held in Emmanuel Church in over thirty-five years. The class to be welcomed into church membership was composed of Mrs. John Sorenson, Miss Nancy Amy, Miss Patricia Gaggs and Mr. William Perry.

The first business to be discussed was a motion made by Mr. Smith and seconded by Miss Templin directing the secretary to write a suitable letter of appreciation to Mr. Fred Meyer thanking him for his gift to the church of the lot adjacent to the church property on the West.

The Rev. O.D. Smith expressed his pleasure at having been with Emmanuel Church for two months this summer and said that he would be glad to come over and conduct services whenever the congregation so desired.

There was some discussion as to the advisability of having a Communion Service the first Sunday in every two months, also special services at Christmas and Easter. The Christmas and Easter services were unanimously favored, but some doubt was expressed as to the monthly service due to the difficulty of heating the church, etc. A motion was made by Miss Templin and seconded by Mrs. Gow that the matter be referred to the ladies of St Agnes Guild for final decision at their next meeting on September 10th.

Miss Templin, treasurer of the Guild, announced that the annual sale held this month would amount to at least $650 though she still lacked the final figures. There being some small collections still to come in. Bishop Huston then complimented the ladies of St. Agnes Guild on the good work they had done in the past, and were still doing.

Mrs. Gow brought up the question of some fine glass windows which had been presented to her by the late Mr. Robert Moran. They are at present stored in the church. The intent had been to have a rose window made for the space above the front door. Mrs. Gow further suggested it might be possible to get a Seattle glazier to make said windows in exchange for the balance of the glass. A motion was made by Miss Templin that the secretary of the Bishop's Committee be instructed to write to the glazier who had made the other windows for the church, for this information. The motion was carried with no further discussion.

A motion was made by Mrs. Gow, seconded by Miss Templin, expressing the thanks of the Committee to the Reverend Mr. Oliver Dow Smith for his service to the church and community this summer, and to Bishop Huston for his presence at Emmanuel Church.

There being no further business the meeting adjourned. Respectfully submitted: Curtis Bailey, Secretary pro tem.

On September 18, 1946, there were eighteen members present including two visitors. Receipts from the annual bazaar came to $667.70. A motion was made and carried that $900 be withdrawn from the bank and placed in a new savings account by the treasurer for a building fund.

A standing vote of thanks was given to Mr. John Sorenson and Mr. Fred Meyer for their generous gifts. A check for $200 was received from the Sorensons and the deed to the lot adjoining our church property was received from Mr. Fred Meyer.

The president suggested that each of the members of the Confirmation Class, the first in 35 years, be honored with a gift of a prayer book from the Guild. A motion was made and carried after the amount was subscribed to by several members during the meeting. The rest has since been subscribed and the prayer books ordered by the secretary. Mrs. Gow moved that the fence be moved to include our new lot and that the Bishop's Committee do the work.

Call for volunteers to make up an altar committee. Mrs. Gow and Mrs. Templin were appointed to head the building committee. It was suggested a contribution of trees as a possible source of lumber for the proposed Guild Hall.

Mrs. Gow offered the holly on her trees for the benefit of the building fund. . . .if someone would cut it without injuring the trees. A committee will volunteer to look after it.

November 5, 1946: The St. Agnes Guild held its meeting at Outlook Inn with Miss Jesse Templin as hostess. Nineteen members and one guest gathered in the pleasant Inn parlor for this annual meeting and election of officers.

June 10, 1947: The Guild met at the home of Mrs. John Sorenson at Dolphin Bay. Sixteen were present and one guest.

The president expressed a desire for us to eventually provide two scholarships for a boy and girl at Camp Huston at Goldbar, Washington. It was also suggested that swimming lessons might be provided for church children, possibly a class formed at (Camp) Orkila.

June 24, 1947: An extra work meeting was held at the Madrona Club House. Nineteen were in attendance and much sewing was accomplished.

It was finally decided to try out the 9:30 a.m. service, June 27 (as that was to be an extra summer service) and see what the results would be.

July 8, 1947: Much work was accomplished. A vote of thanks was expressed to the John Sorensons and the Brinkmans for their devoted service in padding most of the 'kneelers' in the church.

Miss Hart presented the Guild with an exquisite china plate of the Marie Antoinette period.

Aug. 5, 1947: Opening prayers were led by the Rev. O.D. Smith, who followed with a few welcome remarks on the visit of our new Bishop, the Rt. Rev. Stephen Bayne, Jr., on the preceding Sunday.

Aug. 19, 1947: Mrs. Cox reporting for the apron committee said that aprons to the waist and of good material were most popular (for the Bazaar).

Appreciation was expressed for the beautiful dahlias for the decoration of the hall, also for the church, which were contributed by Mr. and Mrs. Glen Rodenberger.

The meeting adjourned for tea at the Bungalow (Cafe), with Mrs. Wright and Mrs. Gauntlett as our gracious hostesses. Twenty were present.

Sept. 9, 1947: The regular monthly meeting of the St. Agnes Guild was held at the home of Mrs. Barton Green in Doe Bay with Mrs. Charles Arnt as assistant hostess. There was a record attendance of 25, including three out-of-town guests.

Pres., Mrs. Curtis Bailey presided and opened the meeting with a beautiful special prayer, followed by the Lord's prayer in unison.

The President announced the glad news that receipts to date from the Summer Sale have reached the amazing total of $572.15.

The President reported on a special meeting of the Bishop's Committee held Sept. 6th at the house of Jessie Templin. To quote the President: 'Your interest in the new Bishop in our little church is like a shot in the arm'.

In a letter to the Warden, he suggested bringing up a church architect to look over the situation. Help from the Missionary fund of the Church-at-large he thought likely. The pledge system was proposed and it was decided to start one.

The Bishop's Committee feel they should be responsible for the expenses of the church. The upkeep of the cemetary, sometimes known as the Episcopal Cemetary, was discussed. The men want to see to cleaning it up.

Mrs. Tvete offered hospitality to Rev. O.D. and Mrs. Smith on the weekends they are here.

Mrs. Trevor Bryant reported on the question of starting a Sunday School. She and Mrs. Arnt are the Committee on Ways and Means. A notice re: the project is to appear in the Orcas Islander.

Mrs. Gaggs was appointed Chairman of the nominating Committee.

Guests were Mrs. Davis of Seattle, Mrs. Cabell of Portland and Mrs. Weldon of Ontario, California.

Oct. 19, 1947: Trevor Bryant reported for the Sunday School Committee. It was decided to try holding Sunday School the first Sunday in November at 10 a.m. in the Madrona Club.

Miss Hart suggested Harvest Home decorations for the church services on Nov. 2. Those who have fall vegetables. . . .were asked to contribute them.

It was agreed to devote the silver offering of today's meeting to the U.T.O. fund. Amt. $7.00.

Nov. 4, 1947: Regular meeting of St. Agnes Guild was held at Outlook Inn with Mrs. Curtis Bailey as hostess. Thirteen members were present.

It was decided some action should be taken to re-interest those who had dropped out and to secure new members.

The treasurer's report was read by Mrs. Wright, who explained her methods of keeping the accounts straight, inviting inspection of the books at any time. She reported a balance of $369.35 in the checking account and $1620 in the savings account and $500 in bonds.

This being the final meeting of the year the President, Mrs. Bailey, read a report of the year's work.

The report of the nominating committee was presented by the Chairman, Mrs. Gaggs. The slate was accepted. The officers for the coming year will be: President, Mrs. Green V.P. Miss Hart, Sec. Mrs. Ammerman and treas. Mrs. Wright. A new office, corresponding secretary was added. Mrs. Bliss was elected to fill it.

Mr. Sorenson said that it was hoped to put the church on a sound financial basis in 1948. This is to be accomplished by the pledge system and the Guild is urged to help promote the plan.

. . .Another meeting is to be held the evening of Nov. 19th at Outlook Inn. Business of vital importance is to be discussed with the Bishop. . .concerning the building of the Parish house, which is a necessary adjunct to the life of the church and has been for a long time very close to the hearts of Guild members.

Dec. 2, 1947: President, Mrs. Green opened with a prayer. We need a candle lighter for the church. It was moved and seconded to purchase a five-foot model and a carton of tapers.

The Bishop will send an architect before Christmas to study our grounds for the hoped-for parish house.

Mrs. Bryant told of her splendid efforts in the newly organized Sunday School. All members so far are from Orcas but it is expected more will be present after Christmas.

Mrs. Gaggs suggested the men have a booth at the Sale to be called 'The Doghouse'. The meeting adjourned, the offering amounted to $14.00.

Those present: Medames Green, Bryant, Updegraff, Clow, L. Burney, Bailey, N. Langell, Larson, Wright, Neth, Young, Hart, Keyes, Soule, Winnie J. Smith, Gow, Lind, Keppler, Mount, Crow, McConnell, Warner, Gaggs, Stewart, Schoen, Albert Wilson, Reed, Henning, Loukes and Ammerman.

Jan. 6, 1948: Regular meeting was held at the home of Miss Jean Crow. After coffee and cream puffs our president opened the meeting at 2:45 p.m. with the Epiphany, collect and the Lord's prayer.

Mrs. Green explained that our part in the building fund has been delayed, that now is the time to pay it because the pledges are to carry on the church work.

Apr. 6, 1948: Guild met at the home of Leland Ammerman, with Mrs. Arney and Mrs. Winne assisting hostesses.

Bishop Bayne opposes selling chances as a means of raising money for the church and articles intended for this purpose will have to be sold.

It was approved that a plaque in memory of Mr. Walter Radford and Mr. Frank Shattuck be erected. It was suggested that we get something useful instead of a plaque. It was moved and seconded to provide the memorial in the form of a gift to the Parish Hall. Mrs. Burney is included in this.

May 4, 1948: St. Agnes Guild met at the home of Mrs. Nova Langell. Treasurer reported $18.80 in the building fund, $145.36 balance in the checking account. Eight dollars is to go to Madrona Club for Sunday School rent. It was decided to doscontinue Sunday School for the summer as the Bryants will not be here. Mrs. Tvete enrolled 17 members. It was suggested that the Sunday School meet in the church during the summer.

Mrs. William, an old parishoner, passed away.

June 1, 1948: President Mrs. Barton Green opened the meeting with a special prayer for world peace followed by the Lord's prayer in unison.

Mrs. Bailey reported on the Sunday School. She expressed deep appreciation of the devoted service of Dr. and Mrs. Trevor Bryant in this work.

The president announced the generous pledge by Mrs. Gow of a memorial fireplace to be built in the new parish house in memory of her husband.

July 6, 1948: There was a note from Dr. Bingham thanking us for baby garments sent to Indians in Fort Yukon.

Mrs. Gaggs asked for the sale in the school gymnasium but the present construction will prevent people from coming so it was decided to ask for use of the Odd Fellow's Hall. It will cost $15.

Mr. Sorenson wants all interested members to meet and discuss plans for the new Parish House on Thursday, 7:30 p.m. at the Madrona Club.

Aug. 17, 1948: Members of the Guold met at the home of Mrs. Max Harrison for a relaxation party after the Sale. The president opened the meeting with a prayer.

The return from the sale was $731.46. Costs were $53.71 making nearly $700 without any chances sold.

Oct. 5, 1948: Mrs. Tvete reports that Mr. Smith asked about $75 for the diocesan house. This drive is a personal obligation. It was moved and seconded that nothing more be given.

Mrs. Tvete suggested that an oil burner be installed in the church. The Sunday School services are much better held there.

Water leaks in the vestry room and repair flashings are needed.

Nov. 2, 1948: Members of St. Agnes Guild met at the home of Mrs. William Burney. The treasurer, Mrs. Wright, gave a final report for the year, stating that we have $3500 altogether. We have had an extremely prosperous year.

We need lights in the church and a committee was appointed to investigate and try to find suitable fixtures.

Mrs. Arnt suggested a note of thanks to Mr. Bryant for installing the furnaces.

The church yard needs leveling.

Jan. 4, 1949: St. Agnes Guild met at the home of Mrs. Hope Stewart with Mrs. Crow assisting hostess. Mrs. Gaggs has been to Mr. Bryant to select lights and he has installed a permanent fixture in the door.

The main subject this month is to do something for the young people of the church. It's necessary that they become more interested. Suggestions for a picnic at Cascade Lake, games Sunday afternoons, or parties were discussed.

Feb. 1, 1949: Mrs. Curtis reported needs for the new school building: namely, two circular tables, about $40, a chemical table, $100, drapes for the lunch room, electric clock and books for the library.

Mrs. Willis is welcomed today. Mrs. Moran has asked us for donations to the March of Dimes. The opinion was expressed not to give to such large, national drives, but rather, locally, as a group. A motion was made to this effect and passed 12 to 2.

March 1949: This is Shrove Tuesday-meaning penitence and confession, it was explained. The treasurer reported a balance of $3198. Mrs. Tvete reported on the Bishop's dinner at Waldheim and suggested that $25 be paid to Waldheim for extra fuel and laundry.

We are now going ahead with building so it is expedient that we all look at the plans now and make any suggestions or comments at this time instead of waiting until after it is finished.

July 5, 1949: There have been no announcements re: bids for the parish house.

Next Sunday 13 are to be confirmed, this is the second class.

It was decided to present the Smiths a $50 bill in a gold envelope in honor of their service and 50th wedding anniversary this fall.

There were 29 members present.

Aug. 2, 1949: St. Agnes Guild met at the home of Mrs. Hawkins. Guests included Mrs. Hartung and Miss Boucher (Mrs. Arney's cousin).

Sept. 6, 1949: The September meeting was held at the home of Mrs. Gauntlett. It was strictly a social meeting to discuss the annual Sale held last month. The treasurer reported $689.22 taken in on the Sale so far. The Four Winds Camp made and bought much of the food. then gave us every cent.

Bids for the Guild hall were too much, but Mr. Sorenson will try to work it out.

The wood in the church yard was sold to Mrs. Redman instead of leaving it to rot.

Oct. 4, 1949: Members discussed donating to the school fund for the teachers' lounge room. It was decided they were asking for too expensive furnishings. It was moved and seconded to give $25.00 for a lamp.

Mrs. Christopher says her husband will help with the Sunday School.

Dec. 6, 1949: The Guild met at the home of Mrs. Curtis Bailey for luncheon.

A friend of Mrs. Bailey gave $300 for our Parish. Mr. John Moran gave $500, the first donation.

Miss Templin is back with us. She gave a talk about her old times reorganizing the Guild with only six members. She will assemble a history of our little church which will be very interesting.

Jan. 9, 1950: A Parish dinner was announced for Jan. 12th.

The president asked for a standing vote of thanks to acknowledge gifts to the church:

3-branch candleabra in memory of Mrs. Galen Burghardt's mother.

Silver wafer box, Mr. and Mrs. L. Burney.

Silk American flag, Mrs. Philip Tvete.

Eagle Crest for flag, Burghardt children.

Mar. 1950: The Guild met at the home of Mrs. John O'Dell in the park, with 17 members and one guest present. Mrs. (Gladys) Curtis called the meeting to order at 3:30 p.m. with the opening prayer.

Since the Parish Hall will not be ready in time to serve Easter breakfast there, as hoped, Outlook Inn will serve breakfast to all who wish it between Easter services on Easter morning.

Apr. 17, 1950: The Guild meeting was held at Mrs. Arnt's home with 25 ladies present.

The president said that the first meeting held in the new hall would be in the nature of a shower. All members to bring dish-towels and other suitable gifts for use in the new kitchen.

Mrs. Larson spoke of the rumor about Dr. Heath leaving the island, but Miss Hart said she had spoken with him about it and he had said there was no truth in it. He did not know how it (the rumor) got started—which was a great relief to us all.

June 6, 1950: St. Agnes Guild met at the home of Mrs. Harding Gow. The discussion was mostly about the Canterbury Players, a group of students from the University who give the plays of St. Francis by Laurence Hausman. They will be on Orcas, June 24th. It is planned to have a picnic in the park where they will present several of their short plays.

June 11, 1950: The July meeting was held at the home of Mrs. Karl Moran.

Miss Hart reported on the Canterbury Players, who arrived amid confusion, but performed at Cascade Lake. They received $36.36 in the silver collection of which half was given to us.

Aug. 7, 1950: The meeting of the St. Agnes Guild was called to order by President Mrs. Gladys Curtis in the Parish Hall.

The treasurer's report gave the final sum made in the Annual Guild Sale $1026.06, a truly astonishing reward.

A letter to John Sorenson, Senior Warden, from James F. Hodges, Diocesan Treasurer in regard to our annual payments on the Parish Hall loan was read. A motion was made and carried to request Mr. Sorenson to find out from Mr. Hodges the entire amount due to Aug. 1, 1952. Mrs. Wright was directed to send a check to Mr. Hodges for that amount. The check was expected to be about $600. Paying it in the entirety would mean a saving to us in interest payments.

Mrs. Stewart announced that she had reached the bottom of the barrel for Sunday Coffee Hour hostesses. A suggestion from someone to discontinue the Coffee Hour was a tempting solution, but Mrs. Max Harrison pumped new blood into the effort by saying that if we could all hear the pleased and enthusiastic comments of visiting church people we'd make a supreme effort to keep on. Therefore the president decided to try the plan of appointing monthly committees.

Nov. 24, 1950: St. Agnes Guild meeting was held at Mrs. Wilson's home.

Mrs. Marge Burney reported that she and Mrs. Culver held the first of our Canasta Parties and turned in $8.50 to the treasury. . . .It was decided to set aside the funds from the parties to buy necessary furnishings for the Parish Hall.

Mrs. Tvete reported that Mr. Pratt had organized the instruction meetings for the Altar Guild.

Mrs. Culver reported that the Sunday School is growing steadily and that there are now enough boys to start a small choir to train them in the processional.

Dec. 1950: The annual December luncheon was held at the home of Mrs. Curtis, president. There were 38 present with Mr. and Mrs. Pratt as guests.

St. Agnes Guild Meets for the First Time in the New Parish Hall

June 1951: Following the reading of a brief devotional message and the Lord's prayer the first business meeting of the St. Agnes Guild in the new Parish Hall was called to order.

Correspondence was read from Mrs. Mary Young, Mrs. V.E. Johnson and Miss Ruth Brown.

July 10, 1951: The meeting was held in the Parish Hall.

Mrs. Curtis Bailey reported for the nominating committee and presented as a ballot Mrs. Vernon Curtis, Pres.; Mrs. L. R. Burney V.P.; Mrs. C.R. Wright, Treas.; Mrs. Karl Moran Sec.; appointments of Mrs. Carol Culver as Publicity Chairman and Mrs. Charles Arnt as special Publicity Chairman for the sale.

A memorial fund for Archie Moore who passed away June 9, was suggested, which would purchase a low brass vase to be placed upon the organ. The vase will be kept filled with flowers as a perpetual memory to Archie Moore and his wife who played the organ while her husband sang for our congregation.

Sept. 11, 1951: The St. Agnes Guild meeting was held at the Parish Hall. It was moved and seconded that $300 be set aside in a savings account to apply upon payment due next year on our debt for the Parish Hall.

A piano was offered for sale to the Parish Hall by Margaret Reid for $100. . . .It was approved that the piano be purchased.

It was carried unanimously to invite Mrs. Melvin to use the Parish Hall for her preschool work this fall without charge for the use of the hall.

Oct. 9, 1951: The meeting of St. Agnes Guild was held in the Parish Hall.

A motion was made and seconded to pay Mr. Clark's bill for $10 for tuning the piano.

It was suggested a note of thanks be sent Mr. Wilbur Johnston for the gift of lumber and labor for the back porch of the hall.

Nov. 13, 1951: The Guild meeting was called to order by Pres. Gladys Curtis.

The recital given by Miss Helen Harrison was well attended. It was an unusual treat for the island people.

The Guild voted to release Father Pratt to his own family for Christmas Eve.

Dec. 4, 1951: There was a discussion on installing a ladder to the attic over the Guild Room to give more space for storage.

Feb. 5, 1952: Pres. Gladys Curtis called the meeting to order.

It was decided to honor Mrs. Melvin at the coffee hour, Feb. 10, in appreciation of her splendid help with the music of the Sunday services.

July 1, 1952: The Guild gave a vote of thanks to Gladys Curtis for the beautiful cake she made for the 25th wedding day celebration for Father and Mrs. Pratt. Also a vote of thanks to Mary Stewart Bailey for the white satin bag presented to Mrs. Pratt.

Aug. 12, 1952: It was moved and carried that we pay our annual payment of $600 on the Parish Hall debt.

The new president of St. Agnes Guild was yet to be chosen.

Chapter Eight

Newspaper Clippings Tell the Story

Following are a number of news clippings taken from the local paper concerning Emmanuel Church and St. Agnes Guild.

The Orcas Islander, Oct. 1946:

The regular meeting of St. Agnes Guild was held Oct. 1, at Outlook Inn. Mrs. Curtis Bailey and Mrs. Charles Bliss were hostesses. . . .

There were 20 members in attendance and lively enthusiasm was shown, especially in the plan for raising funds for the new building project. The dream of this devoted group of women is to erect a parish house on the lot to the west of the church yard, recently given to Emmanuel Church by Fred Meyer. Together with funds on hand and money subscribed for future payments by interested friends, nearly $2000 is credited to this building fund to date.

The work of remodeling the fence on the west side of the church yard so as to include the newly acquired plot of ground has been assigned to the new firm of builders, Winters, Schoen and Clow. The next meeting will be Nov. 5, when Miss Jessie Templin will be hostess as has been her custom ever since the reorganization of St. Agnes Guild at her home in November 1939. This will be the seventh anniversary celebration of this Guild which functioned back in the old days when the Rev.

Mr. Gray established Emmanuel Church more than 50 years ago.

On July 31, 1947, the following item written by Fred Splitstone, author of *Orcas, Gem of the San Juans*, appeared in *The Orcas Islander*:

If this paper reaches you Orcas Island subscribers before noon on Saturday let it remind you that you have just a few hours to get to St. Agnes annual bazaar and tea at the school gymnasium in Eastsound, for that great event takes place from 2 to 5 o'clock this afternoon.

No need to tell what it is like. For years it has been the leading event of its kind on the island. It affords a pleasant meeting place where one can greet old friends, have a cup of delicious tea, and perhaps buy one or several articles that are not found in the stores. That's why everbody goes--unless they forget. This is just to remind you. Do not think you won't be missed. And it is this Saturday from 2 to 5 p.m.

The Orcas Islander, Aug. 7, 1947:

The annual bazaar and tea given by the ladies of St. Agnes Guild at the school gymnasium was a great success. . . .with about $500 worth of sales and a social significance that far exceeded the financial importance of the event. The event afforded a splendid opportunity for summer visitors to get in touch with the finest people on the island and to form a more correct estimate of the quality of the residents. In this way the Guild is a distinct asset to the island as a whole, though its purpose is to restore and mantain Emmanuel Church. It was the principal force that redeemed the church from the state of neglect and disrepair that it had fallen into and is now working to build a parish house adjoining the church.

Excerpted from *The Orcas Islander*, Aug. 12, 1948:

The annual summer sale and tea sponsored by St. Agnes Guild, Aug. 7, was an outstanding success, both socially and financially. More than 200 were in attendance, many off-island visitors timing their vacation so as to include this event. The gross receipts for the day totaled the amazing sum of more than $700.

It was in 1940 that the first of these sales was held in the Madrona Club House under the devoted leadership of Miss Jessie Templin and Mrs. Harding Gow.

The following summer the Guild members, looking for larger quarters found them in the old Beach Hotel, now Outlook Inn, which had long been vacant and had fallen into disrepair. Mr. Fred Meyer having lately become the owner of this old landmark, was preparing to restore it and so kindly allowed the Guild to use it for their 1941 Bazaar.

A much appreciated gift in the form of a painted banner to advertise this sale was made by Mr. Ellsworth Storey, the well known architect who designed and supervised the building of the Observation Tower on Mt. Constitution.
(Excerpted from *The Orcas Islander*, Aug. 11, 1949)

Proceeds from the annual St. Agnes Guild Sale and Tea held Aug. 6, at the I.O.O.F. Hall, surpassed all previous sales according to Mrs. Barton Green, President, $673 was collected to add to the Parish Hall building fund project of the Guild.

The following tribute to Oliver Dow Smith appeared in *The Orcas Islander*, Aug. 18, 1949:

A Tribute

Oliver Dow Smith was known by many of us, and loved by all who knew him. He was a true New Englander to the core, and an adventurer, like a true New Englander, whose ministry covered the Union, from Maine to Olympia. To an unique degree the Church was his life. All he ever cared for was to serve the Church. His interest in personalities and movements was vivid and keen to the very last evening of his life; he felt, as I suppose any true priest does, that the Church had given him all that he had of dignity and stature, and he was a gentleman who never forgot his obligations.

A good many of us knew his quiet way of writing a line of encouragement and praise. He was unstinting in his loyalty to the dioces and to his people, an affectionate and proud friend, and a dear and familiar figure in Convention and Conference. He died completely peacfully, in his sleep, and I have no doubt he is rejoicing in the Great Light where the Church is all and all.

(A paragraph from a letter by the Rt. Rev. Stephen F. Bayne, Jr., Bishop of Olympia, to his clergy, August 4, 1949.)

Chapter Nine

What Emmanuel Church Means to Me

Church attendance has leveled off during the last three years in the United States, after having declined steadily since 1958, according to the Gallup Poll.

In a typical week in 1973, 40 percent of the adults in this country attended church or synagogue. This is the same percentage which attended in 1971-1972. Percentagewise this is 9 percent lower than the recorded 49 percent in 1958.

In 1973, 55 percent of the Roman Catholics attended church in a typical week, compared to 71 percent who attended in 1964.

In contrast, Protestant church attendance has remained stable over the same period of time, with 37 percent of Protestants attending church in an average week during 1973 as compared to 38 percent in 1964.

Specifically, the change in membership of the Episcopal Church from 1952 until 1971 was 487,877. Episcopalians today (1977) number 2,000,900, down 15 percent in the past ten years.

While no single factor can be attributed to the decline in church attendance within the Episcopal Church, it is obvious that such things as the proposed changes in 'The Book of Common Prayer', the ordination of women to the priesthood, as well as the ordination of a homosexual to the priesthood, have all taken their toll in church attendance.

Father Johnson West, Vicar, Emmanuel Church. *(Photo by Willard Stone)*

On the other hand, what is it which inspires loyalty in others to continue attending church services week in and week out, year in and year out?

In an effort to learn the answer to this question locally, members of Emmanuel Church were asked to answer in writing, 'What Emmanuel Church Means To Me'. Their replies follow:

Father Johnson West, Vicar of Emmanuel Church

What does Emmanuel Church mean to me?

It means many things. It means the body of Christ in this Community. It means God with us in the struggle of daily life. It means that even on a remote island His love and concern continue to be manifest and carry his people to the uttermost parts of the world. It means brothers and sisters in Christ, a family who care and forgive and love and support.

In recent years, it has meant also the recognition of a broader family in Christ, as a result of opening its doors to congregations of other heritages. The fact that we share facilities and activities with Roman Catholic and Lutheran congregations opens us to the broader meaning of God With Us. It means living out the realization that that which is given to God, dedicated to God is His, to His glory, not ours to our glory. Thanks be to God for what He has given and what He is doing.

Above all, it means to me, the place wherein I find God always present, ready to answer my prayers, to forgive, to strengthen me and to confirm His promises made through Christ Jesus my Lord and Saviour. Emmanuel Church to me, means life.

Father Jack Marsh, Administrator, St. Francis, Roman Catholic Church.
(Photo by Willard Stone)

Father Jack Marsh, Saint Francis Parish, San Juan Islands

What Emmanuel Church Means To Me

The Sacrifice of the Mass is the most sacred effective contact with God the church enjoys. To be able to celebrate Mass with my Orcas parishioners in the stately and picturesque Episcopal Church in Eastsound is something appreciated by each Catholic and by our many tourists. As a beautiful example of ecuminity it is the pride and joy of both our Dioceses.

The joyful acceptance of our Episcopalian hosts each Sunday morning is a most pleasant experience. Our mutual cooperation in prayer, education, and social functions as planned by the LARC Council, is a giant step toward true, full, Eucharistic, Christian unity.

Besides, the rent is cheap!

Pastor Wm. Chris Boerger, Lutheran Christian Mission of the San Juans.
(Photo by Willard Stone)

Pastor, Wm. Chris Boerger

What Emmanuel Means To Me

I can still remember the first time I was in Emmanuel Church. I had come to Orcas Island to meet with a group of Lutheran Christians. We were to discuss the possibility of beginning a Lutheran congregation and my becoming their pastor. I was on trial since this would be my first parish since graduation from seminary. I remember thinking as I saw the building, if only some of my seminary professors could see this, I would have competition for who would be the pastor of this new mission. The beauty of the location and the warmth of the structure invite the praise of God.

If that had been my only rememberance of Emmanuel, it would be a fond memory. Emmanuel Church is not just the building or the location. Emmanuel is the people of God, called together in this place. I have come to know those people well. It should be said of all churches that the people are the church. It may be more difficult with Emmanuel since we do enjoy a beautiful building and an unmatched location, but here too the people are the Church. As the community of believers gather around the Word of God and the sacraments, it does not just commemorate history but it lives out that history in the lives of its members. One could very easily turn Emmanuel Church into a museum, but to do so would deny the life giving sacrifice of our Lord for which the building was built to recall and renew in the lives of those who gather in the building.

The people of Emmanuel Episcopal Church have demonstrated the courage which can only come from the Spirit in opening their structure to those of the Lutheran and Roman Catholic traditions. I can easily hear the "way of the World" suggesting that this building should be protected and preserved not opened to use by others. When we have something of special value we usually restrict its use rather than invite its use by others. The people of Emmanuel have shown the church at large that we who are of different traditions are not competitors but co-workers in the Lord's service. To do that is to take the gift of Jesus Christ seriously and not withhold for our own gain.

Emmanuel Church holds many special meanings for me. It is here that I began my ministry. It is here that I am ordained into the ministry. It is here that I and the congregation I serve worship, pray, and receive strength from God by His Holy Spirit. But most importantly it is here that the people of God from three traditions have demonstrated and continue to demonstrate that the Spirit given unity which we enjoy can be lived out in our lives. We do not just preach the oneness of Christ, we begin to take shaking steps in living that unity. Emmanuel Church both people and structure are living examples of the love and the power of the Gospel of Jesus Christ.

What Emmanuel Church Means To Me

For me, Emmanuel Church is a place of beginnings.

Every Sunday, Emmanuel offers spiritual refreshment and refueling through the preaching of the Word for the beginning of a new week.

Everytime new people come to Emmanuel there is the beginning of new friendships with Christian brothers and sisters.

Everytime a wedding is performed at Emmanuel there is a joyous beginning for two joined in holy wedlock.

Everytime a baptism occurs at Emmanuel there is a beginning for a new life in Christ.

Everytime there is a confirmation at Emmanuel there is the beginning of a new life in communion with our Lord and Savior.

Everytime a funeral takes place at Emmanuel there is, for the deceased, the beginning of a new life with Christ in his eternal kingdom, as well as a beginning of a new life in faith for those who mourn.

Yes! Emmanuel Church is for me a place of beginnings—beginnings blessed by the Triune God.

—B.H. Goodenough (Lutheran Church)

What Emmanuel Church Means To Me

Never, of a Sunday morning, do I enter my accustomed pew to kneel and worship, but my first prayer is one of thankfulness for the privilege of worshipping in the lovely sanctuary of Emmanuel.

William James has said "To be happy at some point one must have suffered at the same," and this is so for me.

For many years, in small saw mill towns, I had to seek my God in buildings that were far from worshipful. In one town it was the Community Hall, with fold up chairs, stage, and no altar and I would try to discipline myself toward worship by asking: "Is it the senses which draw one to God, such as, stained glass windows, flowers and music; even, in some cases, incense?" No, I knew those were not in themselves the way to God and yet they helped! And I was hungry for help.

There was one evening, in Lent, Good Friday, in another saw-mill town when I went to services in the most barren and ugly little church. It had high ceiling, auditorium seats and no altar. Just a pulpit: No flowers, no candles, no little thoughtfulness of the special time in evidence.

I left the service early, disappointed and emotional; homesick for an attractive, familiar little Church in the town we had just left; crying as I walked home in the darkness.

Is it any wonder I thank the Good Lord each Sunday morning as I kneel in lovely, beloved, worshipful Emmanuel Church and that I realize it is a special privilege to be worshipping there?

—Dorothy Olzendam
(Episcopal Church)

What Emmanuel Church Means To Me

Many churches I have seen and within the walls where I have worshiped my Lord, include the majestic old Trinity Church in Boston, the Diocesan Cathedral in Spokane, the ship's chapel and the open deck of a naval vessel on the open sea during war, palm thatched huts on South Pacific Islands, as well as St Luke's in Wenatchee, St. John's in Olympia and St. Michael's in Yakima.

However, of all the places of worship I have been privileged to bow my head before the Lord, there is one church which stands out above all others and that is Emmanuel Church on Orcas Island, where Clara and I first attended services in 1959. The feeling of warmth, comfort and assurance that God and His Son, Jesus Christ were present and knew that we were there is a feeling which has grown over the years.

The fellowship and friendliness of the entire congregation makes one feel wanted and that he or she is a part of each service. This feeling has continued to increase as the congregation granted me the privilege of further serving the Lord in His house by my lending a helping hand in repairing and remodeling certain sections of the little church made necessary through many years of services.

Then too, our vicar, Father West has also granted me the privilege of taking a more personal part in the service of Emmanuel Church and he has been a great help in making me aware of my own personal direction through God, both within His church and in my daily life.

The beauty of Emmanuel Church with the presence of God and His Son within it, along with the skills and dedication of all those who have built and preserved it for those of us who now attend and love it, make Emmanuel the one church for me among all the church's I have known.　　　—Charles Chapman
(Emmanuel Church)

What Emmanuel Church Means To Me

Having come from a non liturgical church background (Methodist, Dutch Reformed, Presbyterian) I have found the services of Emmanuel Church, based on the Prayer Book, a new and interesting experience and at times inspiring as I became 'adjusted'. Some of the prayers I had known from their use in my former church and my school chapel. From the first I felt a warm welcome and a truly ecumenical spirit as I was allowed to serve on the Bishop's Committee and the Altar Guild. But my greatest joy was the opportunity, due to Father and Mother Benson's invitation, in encouragement and support, once again to teach the Bible and in spite of retirement, to share my training and experience in the field. These classes meant more to me I am sure, than to any of the faithful who studied with me. Emmanuel has truly become my church home.

—Maude Louise Strayer
(Emmanuel Church)

What Emmanuel Church Means To Me

What does Emmanuel Church mean to me? My instant response is 'everything'. Since moving to Orcas Island it's been my home away from home.

First, it means the church itself. That quaint and charming historical structure in Eastsound Village where I go to worship the Lord, to sing His praises and to commune with Him in the presence of my fellow Christians who in turn are my friends and neighbors.

It is always a joy to attend Sunday morning prayer and communion; to meditate in the beauty of the old sanctuary and to be inspired by the beautiful organ music. To meet and enjoy the wonderful fellowship of the parishioners, to meet so many interesting visitors and those wonderful coffee hours is very special.

Emmanuel also means to me, St. Agnes Guild which has played an important part in my life on Orcas Island. It is with a heart warming sense of pride that I am a part of the Guild's outreach which is both local and world-wide.

I was most favorably impressed during my first Guild meeting at the many worthy things this group has accomplished, the monies they have earned by their untiring efforts, particularly through their annual Market Day in July and their used clothing sale each October. It was immediately clear to me that the more we gave the more we received. The results of our diligent efforts are a sure sign that God is blessing us richly.

To have been given the privilege of serving St. Agnes Guild as president was, to me, another blessing. It has afforded me the pleasure of meeting and working with other ladies of the Diocese of Olympia.

The many trips I have made to St. Mark's Cathedral for (FCW) meetings, the days on end spent at the parish hall with my committees to select colors for wallpaper, paints, carpets etcetera, along with the building of an addition to the parish hall to be used as our 'Guild Room', all a labor of love. And the project of my term as president from 1969-1970.

To have been elected an alternate and then a delegate to the Diocesan Convention was both an honor and an education. I shall always be grateful to Emmanuel Church for making this possible.

Two years ago Emmanuel Church became the 'worshiping home' for the Lutheran and Roman Catholic members of Orcas Island, a beautiful example of ecumenism whereby our lovely church building is now enjoyed by even more people of God. As a result of this cooperative union the LARC (Lutheran, Anglican, Roman Catholic) council was formed and again I was blessed with being elected one of three representatives to this council. I find these meetings an exciting exchange between the three congregations who call Emmanuel their church home.

And what a meaningful experience it is to attend the ladies' Bible classes every Monday morning at Benson Hall. The lively discussions and fellowships which are the outgrowth of this class are truly a manifestation of the Holy Spirit.

The close friendships I have been fortunate to form through this unique church and my associations therein, mean more to me than words can convey. I feel privileged indeed, for the many blessings which have come to be mine through Emmanuel Episcopal Church. Praise the Lord.

—Marion T. Burkheimer
(Emmanuel Church)

What Emmanuel Church Means To Me

For my family and myself Emmanuel has become a bridge from the past to the present. Like a bridge its foundations are on solid rock so that all who travel this way are secure in body and refreshed in spirit. My duties as Junior Warden led me to consider the many details surrounding the pysical structure of this old building. It was then I began to learn that many loving hands over many years had built, remodeled, redecorated and cherished this old church building. The loving spirit of those who labored on the structure seem to permeate every board, joint, and nail.

Yes, truly Emmanuel Church is a living bridge so that this generation and those to come may find peace, fellowship and worship as we have.
—Fred Ferguson
(Emmanuel Church)

What Emmanuel Church Means To Me

When asked 'what Emmanuel Church means to me', I think of our coming to Orcas Island and seeing this lovely mission for the first time.

Upon entering the church one immediately has a feeling of warmth, sincerity and beauty.

Roman Catholics and Lutherans alike are welcome to share this church each week. This is where we hold our Masses. To me, this means a great deal.

We pray for the privilege and understanding of these associations and hopefully they will bring us even closer together in Unity.

Yes! I am a Roman Catholic.
—Louise Neal
(St. Francis Parish)

What Emmanuel Church Means and Has Meant in My Life

The threads that bind me to Emmanuel Church are richly interwoven. The first time my husband and I entered this little church by the sea we were enchanted because there were brass lamps hanging from the beams similar to those hanging in the village church in England where my grandparents were baptized. There were other ties. Father Benson, the vicar at Emmanuel, had been rector of the church in Colorado when we had moved there twenty-five years before, and he had baptized our younger daughter. Now, as we contemplated ending our long careers of college teaching, he encouraged us to follow him to the land of blue water, snow-capped peaks, and tall fir trees, back to the land of my birth.

We came, but too late. When we arrived on Orcas Island to stay, Father Benson was already in the hospital in Port Angeles, his life ebbing as our new home arose. Before our move I had seen photographs of Father West in the island newspaper and had wondered what part he would play in our lives. Now he and his lovely wife June were our close neighbors and soon became even closer friends. My husband was elected to the Bishop's Committee of Emmanuel Church four months after our arrival and he looked forward to supporting the work of Father West in all the years ahead.

The years, however, were short indeed. Eight months after our arrival on the island, my husband came home from a meeting of the Bishop's Committee to tell me that Father Benson had died. We planned to attend his service the following Tuesday. Two days later, I awoke to find my husband had also died, suddenly and peacefully. His service was held the day before Father Benson's. Mother Benson and her daughter were in attendance. My daughter and I attended Father Benson's service. Thus Mother Benson and I began the long journey through bereavement together, watching one another's light each evening across the waters of Eastsound, she nestled among the rocks from which Father Benson had loved to launch his boat, I high among the crags from which my husband had often exclaimed, "You couldn't have brought me to a more perfect spot." We were invited out together, she and I, and when we parted at the end of the evening the sight of that indomitable little figure trotting down the path to her empty home sustained me as I drove home to mine.

Now, at the time when the life I had known and dreamed of was demolished, the people of Emmanuel Church flowed about me, sustaining me, making me a part of the family that is the Church. Such a treasure of personalities and experiences flourishes in this small group! The Wests became the brother and sister for whom I had always longed. Charles and Clara Chapman guided me through the shoals of completing my home and Clara, who had used my design book in her weaving long before she knew me, inspired me as I struggled to resume my careers of writing and painting. Maude Louise Strayer, intrepid headmistress and climber of Alps, assured me in her eighties that life for a woman alone can be rewarding. And Dorothy and Rod Olzendam, who had known the experience of grief in their own rich lives, enveloped me in love and understanding, including me in wonderful parties and in quiet moments at Freedom Point watching the ferries glide by, providing a vision of the beauty and dignity with which life can be lived.

I have loved the Episcopal Church since I was sixteen, when I first entered St. John's Cathedral in Denver for the midnight service on Christmas Eve. I loved the little church at the foot of the Rockies where I was confirmed, Grace Church in New York where I lived at the Girls' Club, the magnificent cathedrals of Europe and England about which I lectured throughout my teaching career. All of these threads are woven together in this chapel on the rocks where the breezes from the sea caress the windows and the call of gulls punctuates the litany, and where people from all over the world bring the fruits of their lives to lay upon the altar. —Marjorie Bevlin
(Emmanuel Church)

Chapter Ten

St. David's Church
Friday Harbor, San Juan Island

(From an unpublished history of St. David's Church)

Foreword

In April of 1973 Mrs. William E. Murphy suggested to Father Edward D. Leche, vicar of the San Juan Islands Mission, that inasmuch as many years had passed since the founding of St. David's, that it would be in order to honor those who have pioneered the Episcopal Mission in Friday Harbor. Father Leche and others approved the suggestion, and the idea was expanded to include a written account of St. David's early beginnings. Accordingly, Mrs. Murphy called together a group who had been among those who had been instrumental in organizing the early church. Pictures and other significant items were collected, and important events were recalled.

To those early pioneers and to successive generations of worshipers and workers this history of St. David's is sincerely dedicated.

Frances M. Seels
July 7, 1975

In the fall of 1950, at the request of the Rt. Rev. Stephen Fielding Bayne, Jr., Bishop of Olympia, Father Cotton made his way to the town of Friday Harbor. His assignment was to look into the possibility of establishing an Episcopal Mission on San Juan Island.

Father Cotton met first with the island physician, Dr. Malcolm G. Heath who arranged for Father Cotton to meet and talk with Mrs. Frances Baker.

*'For where two or three are gathered in my name there am
I in the midst of them.'* Matthew 18:20

Following her meeting with Father Cotton Mrs. Baker got in touch with other Episcopalians. The prospect of having an Episcopal Church on San Juan Island was greeted with enthusiasm.

Christmas Episcopal Church Service Sunday

Episcopal services by Rev. Fr. G.F. Pratt commemorating the birth of Christ will be held in the Valley Church, Sunday evening at 8:00 o'clock. Holy Communion will be celebrated, and any persons who wish are invited to join. It will be a candle-light service, and there will be a sermon.

At the time, Father George Foster Pratt of Abbotsford, British Columbia, was holding services on Orcas and Lopez Islands. A group of interested women invited Father Pratt to tea at the home of Mrs. Mike Arnold where plans were made for Father Pratt to conduct services on San Juan Island.

By February of 1951 the necessary arrangements had been made. Services would be held weekly in the Valley Church. (It was actually San Juan Valley Community Church, formally Emmanuel Presbyterian Church, built in 1882.)

In the late forties the church had been restored as a community project under the leadership of Mrs. Ella Dightman. It was cleaned and polished once again by the Episcopalian group. The oil heater was made ready for use, the kerosene lamps cleaned and filled and the old organ was tested and found trustworthy.

Incidentally, the little mouse who lived in the organ would come out each Sunday evening and sit quietly cleaning his whiskers and enjoying the services.

In the beginning, Frances Baker and Mary Reed accepted the responsibility for caring for the altar for which they provided linen and altar ware from their respective homes. Father Pratt would bring the Traveling Communion Set when he came.

On February eighteenth at eight o'clock in the evening the first service was held.

In the fall of 1952 notices of the Episcopal Church Services began to appear in the *Friday Harbor Journal*. The September eleventh issue carried this item:

'I am the true vine,
and you are the branches.
He who dwells in me,
as I dwell in him
bears much fruit:
for apart from me
you can do nothing.
John 15:5

Sometime during those early years Reg Boddington, who was a member of the OPALCO staff, wired the Valley Church for electric lighting at his expense. The Guild minutes for November, 1953 note that 'Mrs. Reed loaned an electric heater to make the vestry room more comfortable.'

Although the women of the church had been active from the beginning, the first available written records of their activities are the minutes of the meetings of St. Anne's Guild. The first, at hand, dated September 10, 1953. St. Anne's Guild was an active and dedicated group who ministered to the needs of the San Juan Mission, and to other Missions as well; St. Stephen's Mission at Fort Yukon, Alaska, was one.

In 1953, Father Pratt's last year as Vicar of the Island Missions proved to be a busy and productive year. In April of 1953 special Easter services were held.

On Thursday, April 2, 1953, the following notice appeared in the Friday Harbor Journal:

Easter Services in the Valley Church

On Easter Eve (Sat. next) Holy Baptism will be held at 5:00 o'clock by the Rev. G.F. Pratt of the Episcopal Church. Anyone desirous of having their child or themselves baptized at this time please telephone 1154 and leave name.

On Easter morning, Apr. 5th, Holy Communion will be celebrated at a sunrise service. All are invited to participate in this important feast of the Christain world: the resurrection of Jesus Christ.

In July Father Pratt began a series of Confirmation Classes which he held in the homes of members of the congregation on Saturday evenings. Other Confirmation Classes were held in the following homes: Mrs. Ella Dightman on July 9th, Mrs. Vincent Moore, August 6th, Mrs. Connor Reed, August 20th and Mrs. Vincent Moore, August 29th.

Instruction having been completed everyone looked forward to a visit from Bishop Stephen Bayne and on September 3rd the following item appeared in the *Journal*:

Bishop Bayne, Episcopal (Bishop) of the Diocese of Olympia, will visit Friday Harbor Sunday next, Sept. 6, and at 8:00 P.M. will hold services in the Valley Church. Rev. Fr. George F. Pratt, Rector in charge, will present a class for confirmation to the Bishop at this time. Bishop Bayne will address the congregation, and the general public is cordially invited to hear the message.

As the year drew to a close, news of a proposed change was received in Friday Harbor: Fr. Pratt and Fr. Johnson West, of Whatcom County were to exchange parochial duties. The plans were for Fr. West to reside on Orcas Island, and to serve as full-time vicar for the Island Missions. In due course, St. Anne's Guild met to consider how best to express their deep feelings of appreciation to Fr. Pratt. As a token of their appreciation the women gave him a gift of a beautiful shrub.

Those who were members of Fr. Pratt's congregation tell how, as he preached, Fr. Pratt would walk up and down the aisle, occasionally pausing to sit beside one person or another. They remember him as a warm, likeable person.

On February 4, 1954, news of Fr. West's approaching arrival appeared on the front page of the *Friday Harbor Journal*:

New Episcopal Vicar for this Church District

According to a mainland news item the Rev. Johnson E. West, of the Episcopal Church of Whatcom County, will succeed the Rev. George F. Pratt. Rev. West has been appointed to serve as Vicar of the San Juan Islands. The West family will move from Everson to their new residence near Doe Bay. He will serve the congregation of Emmanuel Church at Eastsound, the congregation on San Juan Island, and the residents of Lopez and Shaw Islands.

On Friday, February 12th, the members of St. Anne's Guild greeted Fr. and Mrs. West with a welcoming luncheon.

Father George Pratt Writes

Dear Mrs. Seeles:

First, in answer to your recent letter, please let me convey our sincere regrets to Fr. and Mrs. Leche that we are unable to be with you June 18. On that day our new four-lane highway bridge over the Fraser River is to be opened and I promised long ago to give the blessing on this occasion. We could get to Friday Harbor by flying but that would be expensive.

I began my work in the San Juan Islands in the late Fall of 1950 and conducted services on Lopez and Orcas.

My first service on San Juan Island was held Sunday, February 18, 1951 at 8 p.m. This service and all succeeding ones during my tenure were held in the Community Church quite a distance from Friday Harbor. Our congregations were small and averaged 12-15. You will have the names of those most active at the time. Reg Boddington was the Warden and indeed proved a fine active churchman.

In good weather I used the plane from Orcas, but of course, had to use the ferry in winter and bad weather. Oftentimes I stayed over until Tuesday using Monday as a day for visiting the families on the Island. I cannot forget the funny little hotel near the harbor where I stayed most of the time, and the rope attached to each room via the window in case of fire. The good keepers of that day always offered a warm welcome.

Services were observed weekly until my transfer to the Whatcom County Missions, and Father West and I exchanged parochial duties.

I trust these few notes will be helpful to you.

Mrs. Pratt joins in wishing you all a happy and blessed Anniversary. We wish we could be with you.

Faithfully yours,
Geo. Foster Pratt

Significant events were continuing to happen in 1956. In March of this year members of the Guild were delighted by the opportunity to send a gift to the newly arrived baby, Deborah West. In July, Ted Lottsfeldt, the first of a number of successive seminarians arrived to conduct instruction classes for six weeks. Shortly after Father West's wishes to become an Air Force Chaplain were realized and on October 4th, the *Friday Harbor Journal* announced the coming of a new Vicar.

Rev. Glion Benson New
Episcopal Vicar for County

Galen Burghardt of Eastsound, Sr. Warden of Emmanuel Church Mission, states that he is happy to announce the appointment of the Rev. Glion Benson to serve as Vicar of the San Juan Mission of the Episcopal Church.

Mr. Benson comes to the Mission from Sedro-Woolley where he has served for the past several years, and he and Mrs. Benson will take up residence in the newly purchased vicarage. . .They are not strangers to the community as the Bensons have spent several vacations on Orcas Island, and have visited on San Juan and Lopez.

On Friday evening, October 26, 1956, at Emmanuel Church in Eastsound Father Benson was installed as Vicar of the San Juan Islands Mission. The office of Institution was conducted by Bishop Stephen Bayne with members from Orcas, Lopez and San Juan Islands participating. The following week St. David's Church in Friday Harbor entertained Father and Mrs. Benson and Archdeacon Walter McNeil at dinner.

His ministry now officially begun, Father Benson continued a busy schedule already under way. As described in the magazine *FORTH*:

From Eastsound, Orcas Island, the Rev. Glion T. Benson, vicar of the San Juan Islands Mission, island hops by plane and boat, conducting Sunday morning services at his home base, Emmanuel Church, Eastsound; an afternoon service at Lopez Island's Grace Parish; and an evening service at St. David's, Friday Harbor. Sometimes he goes inland for special services at historic Valley Church in the interior of San Juan Island. His week is divided in the same manner among parishoners of the various islands, an arduous schedule which may call for missed meals and long hours.

Oftentimes his transportation was provided by various boat owners among the parishoners. Whenever feasible Father Benson remained in Friday Harbor over night. The advertisement in the *Journal* read:

Episcopal Church services each Sunday at the Chapel on Spring Street. Sunday School 11:30 a.m.; Evening prayer— 7:30 p.m. The Rev. Glion Benson, vicar. The vicar will be at the Parish Rooms each Monday until the ferry.

With the arrival of a full time Vicar, a number of changes were in store for the San Juan Islands Mission. Events moved in rapid succession and it became possible to provide additional services for Friday Harbor. In March the Bishop's Committee met with St. Anne's Guild to outline a program which was being set up for the Mission as a whole: the center of operations was to be Emmanuel Church in Eastsound with all Mission finances (receipts and disbursements) being handled from there. The estimated project budget was $9000.00. Other plans included the taking of a denominational census in all islands. Arrangements were made to enlist members of the Episcopal and Presbyterian congregations to carry out the project.

In June Father West met with the Guild and other members of the congregation to distribute the census forms, and to discuss the possibility of opening an office in Friday Harbor. He proposed to rent a suite of rooms formerly occupied by Dr. T.H. Judge (the suite occupied by 'Barbara's Boutique') for $20.00 a month. Everyone was enthusiastic; friends, members and the Guild advanced four months rent, and the deal was closed.

In June, in response to Father West's suggestion, the congregation selected St. David's Episcopal Church as the name for their Friday Harbor Church.

Once again members of the church set about cleaning, polishing and decorating and by August the rooms were ready for use. However, it wasn't until early in 1955 that the worship services were held in the large front room.

On August 26, 1954, the *Journal* announced the formal opening of St. David's Parish Office and Meeting Rooms:

> "Sunday, Aug. 8, the formal opening and blessing of St. David's Parish office and meeting rooms occurred. These rooms are those formerly used by the late Dr. T.H. Judge, situated on the main street of Friday Harbor.
>
> The Rev. Johnson E. West officiated, following evening service at the Valley Church. The choir from Emmanuel Church, Eastsound, added to the occasion by singing numerous selections 'a Capella'. A young acolyte from the same church assisted the Rev. Mr. West. Dr. Roger Loring was present and made appropriate remarks about the history of the building. Dr. Malcolm Heath spoke briefly, stressing 'Searchers after Truth'. . . .The Rev. Gordon

St. David's Sunday School class was held in a Friday Harbor store front prior to construction of the church. *(Photo by Bill Stephens)*

Winson of the Friday Harbor Presbyterian Church closed the speech-making by eloquently stressing 'Fellowship'.

The Hostesses were members of St. Anne's Guild of this Parish.

The year 1957 was to bring new and wonderful developments. The congregation of St. David's was already talking about building a church building, and were casting about for a suitable location. A building fund had been started: the Guild minutes for February 15th show a deposit of $115.00 to this fund.

News of the 'Voyaging Vicar of the San Juans' had spread abroad, and Episcopal Churchwomen in the Tacoma-Seattle area made him a gift of a boat. It was christened the 'ROYAL

CROSS' on April 11th, 1957. An article in *FORTH* magazine reports:

> The vicar's split-second schedule recently was simplified by a 26-foot, 25 H.P. diesel powered Navy whaleboat, the gift of the Daughters of the King in Tacoma-Seattle area. Blessed and recommissioned to God's service by the Rt. Rev. Stephen Bayne, Jr., Bishop of Olympia,, the boat was christened 'Royal Cross' after the emblem of the Daughters of the King.
>
> Boats are not new to either the vicar or his 'first mate.' As a girl in England, Mrs. Benson learned to love the sea during vacations aboard sturdy fishing vessels off the coast of Wales. Mr. Benson sailed the Great Lakes in his boyhood and youth.

The vicar made his first trip to Friday Harbor on the Royal Cross May 26th. On this same date the Episcopal and Presbyterian congregations met together in the Presbyterian Church to participate in a baccalaureate service, conducted by Father Benson, for the graduating high school seniors: the service having been designed by Father Benson for the Friday Harbor Public Schools.

One of the persons actively involved in the building of St. David's from the beginning was the Rev. Canon Walter W. McNeil, Archdeacon of the Diocese of Olympia, who, among other things, conducted worship services from time to time. During the summer of '57, on a particularly hot Sunday morning while Archdeacon McNeil was delivering a sermon in the Chapel on Spring Street, Mr. D.W. Fletcher, a member of the congregation, noted that the Archdeacon's face was becoming extremely red.

He observed to those near him, 'That man's going to have apoplexy.'

At the conclusion of the sermon he rose to his full six-foot-three inches of height and announced that he would give a plot of land to the people of St. David's provided they would put a church on it. Mr. Fletcher was as good as his word and on October 11, 1957, lots 38, 39, 40 and 41, at the corner of Marguerite and Park Streets were transferred to the Diocese of Olympia in trust for the building of St. David's Episcopal Church.

Then came the question of where to get the money to erect the building. The men of the congregation felt sure that the San Juan County Bank would lend them the money. As Father Benson recalls it: several of the men including himself, Mr. Oliver Sandwith, Mr. William Kilpatrick of Friday Harbor and Dr. James Hodges of Seattle, approached Mr. Cecil Carter, President of the bank. Mr. Carter took them back to a small office and after a brief conversation Mr. Carter said, "How much do you want? Whatever you need you can have at 5% interest."

Having determined the amount needed, Mr. Carter, using one finger, typed up the note.

Incidentally, the note was paid on time and in full with no financial help from outside the community. No small part of the money was raised by the guilds. In October of this year (1957) a second guild was formed. A group of women met Friday evening, October 4th, in the home of Lavina Murphy, and organized St. Margaret's Guild.

Work got under way immediately. Oliver Sandwith drew up plans for the building (since remodeled for use as the vicarage). Excavations were completed and the foundation laid. Sometime during this period plans were made to place a tall cross, carved from a single tree, near the entrance to the church. As it turned out, Mr. Chip Sikes bought the tree at Roche Harbor, Mr. Fred Johnson carved the cross, and Mr. Nicholas Skottowe painted it. It was lifted into place sometime during the summer of 1958.

Friends in Seattle continued to be interested in St. David's. A gift of a beautiful candelabra was received with the inscription:

The dedication of St. David's Church, Friday Harbor on San Juan Island, June 16, 1963. Left to right: Bishop Lewis, Archdeacon, Walter McNeil, Father Glion Benson, Father John Dirks, James Marner and Dr. Hodges.

Given to St. Andrews By The Lake, Seattle, 1946—Passed on with love, to St. David's, when a new and larger church made larger altar appointments necessary.

Fortunately, throughout its early years St. David's was blessed with competent, dedicated Lay Readers and devoted Acolytes.

The early months of 1958 proved busy ones with members and friends of St. David's continuing to work and worship together. By June the new building was completed. The carpenter work, including the beautiful finishing work on the interior of the new building was done by members of the congregation. This included the altar and pews. On June 22nd the first service was held in the new building.

In October an Altar guild was formed and arrangements were made for a member from each guild to attend the altar and clean the church each month.

A truly elegant bazaar was put on by the St. Margaret and St. Ann Guilds in November of 1958. Held in the Study Club, the doors opened at 11:00 a.m. 'for an all day festival for Christmas shoppers.' One of the special features was a plate lunch for 75 cents.

In 1959 two events of particular significance were reported in the *Friday Harbor Journal*. Number one appeared in the January 8th issue:

> In celebration of the Epiphany, members of St. David's Episcopal Parish met to hold Communion Service on the eve of January 6th. Following the Communion Service the yearly Parish meeting and dinner were held with the Rev. Walter W. McNeil officiating. A Parish Committee was set up to handle the business affairs of the church. The members serving this committee are Charles Taylor, Chairman and representative to the Bishop's Committee. . . Oliver Sandwith, Vice Chairman and building Chairman; Burt Winne, Clerk; Nick Skottowe, William Murphy, and Al Johnson.

Number two appeared in the September 3rd issue:

> Sunday morning, September 6th, at ten o'clock Bishop Stephen Bayne will consecrate the church building of St. David's Episcopal Church. .This event is looked to with a great deal of joy by members of St. David's Congregation as Churches are not officially consecrated until they have been paid for.
>
> This will be Bishop Bayne's last visit to the San Juan Islands as he leaves the Diocese in December to become Executive Officer of the Lambeth Conference with his office in London, England.
>
> Accompanying Bishop Bayne to Friday Harbor will be the Rev. Walter W. McNeil, Archdeacon of the Diocese.
>
> The Order of Confirmation will be held for a Confirmation Class following the Consecration ceremonies. The Order of Holy Communion will follow the Confirmation ceremony after which the congregation and their guests

Grace Church on Lopez Island, like other San Juan Island Episcopal Churches, was built with the help of many dedicated islanders.

will go to the home of Mr. and Mrs. W.T. (Scotty) Moffat for the coffee hour.

In the Years to Come

In the years to come—

The members and friends of St. David's congregation would construct yet another building: the beautiful church building presently in use.

Father Pratt would receive the designation—'Canon of Honor'—1964

Johnson E. West, Lt. Colonel, Retired, would return to Eastsound as vicar of Emmanuel Church—1974

Father Benson would be designated—The Rev. Canon Glion T. Benson, Missioner—April 11, 1964

The Rev. Edward D. Leche would become vicar of San Juan Islands Mission—1967.

Epilogue

by
Mary Jane Leche

Father Glion Benson continued to serve St. David's as vicar, but his burden was lightened when a young deacon, the Rev. John Armstrong Dirks, was sent to Friday Harbor to share in the work there.

Father Dirks was a deacon. He arrived in 1961, but was ordained to the sacred priesthood in December, 1961, by Bishop William Fisher Lewis in the Presbyterian Church in Friday Harbor.

With an assistant Priest now resident on San Juan Island plans went rapidly ahead to build a new church building on the corner property adjacent to the existing building.

Mr. John Dickson, a member of the congregation, was architect for the new building. Again, much of the labor was furnished by men of the congregation. The new church was dedicated on the first Sunday after Trinity on June 16, 1963, by Bishop Lewis.

Father Dirks was called to be an assistant at St. Mary's Church at Lakewood (Tacoma), Washington. He and his family left Friday Harbor in November of 1964 for his new assignment.

Another young deacon, the Rev. John B. Rowe, was sent to assist Father Benson on July 1, 1965, but remained on the island only three months.

Following Father Glion Benson's retirement, the Rev. Edward D. Leche, a priest with twelve years experience, primarily in the mission field in the diocese, was assigned by Bishop Ivol Ira Curtis to become Vicar of the San Juan Islands Mission on April 1, 1967.

The original church building was used for Sunday School and as a parish hall, following the completion of the new church. When housing for the Leche family could not be found, it was decided to complete the daylight basement area beneath the new church for parish hall use and to add to the old church on each end and across the front to provide housing for Father Leche and his wife and four children who ranged in age from eleven years to five months.

A Mount Vernon designer, William Davidson, drew up plans for the new vicarage which included the vicar's office. In March of 1968 the Leche family gratefully moved into their new quarters.

Inevitable changes came rapidly to the San Juan Islands as well as to the rest of the country and to the national church as well as to St. David's. Changes are still occurring.

Father Leche served the islands without an assistant (although Father Benson helped immeasurably by taking a number of services, especially on Orcas Island) until Father Johnson West returned to become Vicar of Emmanuel Church, in Eastsound on August 1, 1974.

The 'Royal Cross' became the property of the Kaiser Foundation on Orcas Island and Father Leche used what money he realized from the sale of his former home as a down payment on a 19-foot inboard-outboard Reinell, the 'Seraph', and undertook a personal loan to make possible the more rapid means of circulating among his scattered flock on San Juan, Lopez, Shaw, and Waldron Islands, and until 1974, Orcas Island.

Father Edward D. Leche, Vicar of San Juan Islands Mission.

A much needed narthex was added to the front of the new church, and dedicated to the 'glory of God, and in loving memory of Frank Blumberg,' by Bishop Curtis, on August 5, 1972.

In 1974, a portico in front of the basement doors was added and landscaping efforts, largely undertaken by Captain and Mrs. James A. Lovering, have increasingly beautified the property.

The lovely hatch cover altar was moved out from the sanctuary wall in 1972 in accordance with the changing liturgical practice. The Women of St. David's no longer divided into guilds, purchased and had installed a lovely red carpet in the sanctuary and down the center aisle of the nave. A new altar rail was provided at this time enlarging the sanctuary and allowing more people to be communicated at one time.

An eight-foot Alaska cedar log was transformed into a magnificently carved Christus Rex by the skilled hands of Lopez artist, Bruce Collman, and painted by Mrs. Collman. The Christus Rex was a gift of Mr. and Mrs. George Moseley to the 'glory of God and in loving memory of their son, David Craigin' and was blessed at the midnight service on Christmas Eve, 1972.

The women of the church look forward soon to decorating the parish hall in a more homelike fashion. The hall has already proven a tangible witness to the community at large of the congregation's concern for its needs (providing a meeting place for pre-school youngsters, Girl Scouts, Alcoholics Anonymous, licensing officer for the Department of Motor Vehicles, etc.) and to other Christians who have enjoyed the facility (St. Francis Roman Catholic Congregation and Daily Vacation Bible School with the students and staff from the Presbyterian Church).

A faithful organist and outstanding musician, Mrs. Dianna Marshall, moved to Mount Vernon in the fall of 1974. She played on the church's first reed organ and then on the new electric organ which was purchased from the Presbyterian Church.

The vicar and congregation of St. David's give thanks to Almighty God for his many blessings in the past, and look forward to serving Him and His many children on San Juan Island in this bicentennial year and in the years to come.

> *. . .Faith, Hope, Charity,*
> *but the greatest of these is charity.*
> *1 Corinthians 13: 13*

Parish Gifts

Through spring, 1955, furnishings for the Parish rooms were being acquired and completed in one way or another. A bed-davenport was provided as a convenience for the Vicar's overnight stays. The men completed the building of a small altar and portable altar rails, and the women finished the altar linens.

Gifts from friends in other areas rounded out the essential requirements; two cruets for Communion use were received from 'The Traveler's Gift Shop' in Bellingham, folding chairs and a dossal were donated by friends in Seattle, to mention but a few.

By May worship services were being held regularly in the Parish Chapel, and St. Anne's Guild voted to discontinue paying for electricity and oil for Valley Church.

Throughout 1955-1956 St. David's continued to grow and flourish. During this period Mrs. Mingst of St. Andrews in Seattle, (formerly a resident of Friday Harbor) contributed a church library as a memorial to her son, Peter. Another gift was a sign which was hung above the entrance to the Chapel.

Acknowledgments

Thanks go to all those who participated in providing firsthand information, reference material and pictures as sources of material for this book.

The Rev. Canon Glion T. Benson, Missioner
The Rev. Edward D. Leche, Vicar
The Rev. Canon George Foster Pratt

Remson Apgar
Frances Baker
William Baker
Lenna Blumberg
Jean Benson
Staff of the *Friday Harbor Journal*
Barbara Hovey
Louise Kilpatrick
William Kilpatrick
Keturah King
Mary Jane Leche

Dianna Marshall
Lavinia Murphy
William Murphy
Clara Murphy
Warren Russell
Oliver Sandwith
Virginia Sandwith
Agnes Skottowe
Nicholas Skottowe
Agnes Thompson

Chapter Eleven

Grace Church, Lopez Island

Those who attend Grace Church on Lopez Island, will long remember Father Benson's untiring assistance over the years in helping to build this picturesque little church.

Says "Mother" Benson: "We managed to build Grace Church without having to borrow any money. I recall that during the construction of the parish hall that they wanted the inside of the hall to appear as though there were tree trunks standing there with light showing between them, just as though they were actually growing outdoors. I remember this because for three years during our summer vacations, Father Benson and I would drive all around Lopez Island looking for cedar trees we could use in the construction of parish hall. Then one November day a big storm came up and four huge tree trunks washed up on the beach just below the church.

"I might add that the men lost no time hauling those logs to the only sawmill on Lopez Island where they were sawed into lumber and used to construct the parish hall. God had heard our prayers and for all practical purposes He had delivered those tree trunks practically to our church doorsteps."

Chapter Twelve

Emmanuel Church's Ecumenical Goals

In keeping with the Ecumenical Council of Churches throughout the world to promote world-wide Christianity the Rt. Rev. Robert H. Cochrane, D.D., Bishop of Olympia of Western Washington has suggested the following Diocesan goals for the years 1976-1980:

1. A strong and unified prophetic voice from the Diocese speaking God's Word to the issues facing our state and nation.

2. An active outreach or CSR committee in every congregation of the Diocese that shall report annually on its activities to our Diocesan CSR Committee.

3. The establishment of an active Diocesan program to meet the needs of the elderly of our Diocese and to aid the congregations in such ministry.

4. The strengthening of our ecumenical relationships at both the Diocesan and congregational levels.

5. A 25% increase in the number of Baptisms and Confirmations and a 50% increase in average church attendance throughout the Diocese.

6. The establishment of the half-tithe ($1 a week for every $1000 of annual income) as the average level of giving throughout the Diocese.

7. The establishment of at least one new mission congregation and/or one new area of mission activity each year.

8. The establishment of a creative and workable plan for the fair and effective use of all the clergy resources of the Diocese, stipendiary and non-stipendiary, parochial and non-parochial.

9. The establishment of the Holy Eucharist as the act of worship in every congregation of the Diocese with at least two celebrations each Sunday and two weekday celebrations each week.

10. An active Prayer Group in every congregation of the Diocese.

11. An annual Quiet Day, Retreat, Preaching or Healing Mission for every congregation in the Diocese.

12. Increased participation by the congregations in such corporate Diocesan acts of worship in our Cathedral as: Cathedral Day and All Saints and Ascension Day Eucharists.

Ascension Day Eucharists

Some of the steps taken at this time by the vestry of Emmanuel Church to carry out Bishop Cochrane's suggested Diocesan Goals include:

1. Interdenominational Study Groups.

2. Women's Bible Study Group which meets every Monday morning at Benson Hall.

3. Men's 'Brown Bag' Bible Study Group, non-denominational, which meets every Thursday at 12 noon at Benson Hall.

4. Special courses are held periodically under the direction of the College of Christian Concerns. Subjects have covered 'Dying' and 'Edge of Adventure', which concerns itself with Christian growth.

5. Emmanuel Church was first in the community to make a meeting place available to the island's Senior Citizen's group.
6. Other Church contributions to the community at large include the use of its parish hall for group meetings such as Alcoholics Anonymous, Alanon, (children of alcoholics), Art Classes, Childrens' Dance Classes, etc. Charges for the use of the hall are nominal and in some instances they are waived, depending upon the occasion.

According to Harold and Margaret Gaggs, who first began coming to Orcas Island during the summer months in 1936, as far back as the early forties the Catholic Clergy had been invited to use Emmanuel Church for its services. However, in those years it was against the Catholic principle for the Catholic denomination to hold its services in any Episcopal Church.

Margaret Gaggs recalled an incident which occurred some twenty years ago: "A young Catholic lad who was visiting with us on Orcas Island wanted to see the inside of Emmanuel Church so I took him on a tour of the church. As we were coming out of the chapel the little Catholic boy said somewhat sheepishly, 'Boy, wait till I tell Sister Mary that I went into an Episcopal Church.' "

Since those days the Catholic Church has undergone a considerable change. In 1962 Pope John XXIII inaugurated a new era in the history of the Roman Catholic Church by summoning the second Vatican Council to meet. As a result of this universal change in the Catholic Church's policy, Catholic services have been held in Emmanuel Church since 1975.

As a direct result of this sharing of church facilities three denominations have formed a nine-member council which is composed of three members from each of the following churches: Episcopal, Roman Catholic and Lutheran. Its purpose is to provide an on-going instrument whereby selected members of the three congregations may meet to discuss concerns of the congregations they represent. They also assist the clergy in formulating plans and programs which may further the Gospel of Christ Jesus within the Orcas Island Community. The council stands ready to meet with representatives of the Community Church and other Christian bodies as may later be formed.

As its 'official voice' the council publishes a monthly bulletin called the LARC (Lutheran, Anglican and Roman Catholic) in which are published such things as the hours of the weekly services of the three denominations LARC represents; important dates of church related events and meetings; general church news, et cetera.

Chapter Thirteen

Liturgical Changes: Are They Good or Bad?

Recent years have seen a number of liturgical and Prayer Book changes within the Episcopal Church, several of which have caused considerable controversy among the ecclesiastical hierarchy and members of the church. Dedicated Episcopalians throughout the nation have expressed concern over these changes. Here on Orcas Island, Roderic Marble Olzendam, coauthor of this book, himself a dedicated Episcopalian, was baptized in 1892 and has been a lay reader since 1910. A recipient of the Bishop's Cross 'for outstanding services to church and state', Olzendam has taken a number of steps to make known his own feelings on some of these changes.

In his autobiography, *Liberty's Grandson*, the author expressed his innermost feelings about the proposed changes in the 'Book of Common Prayer' as follows:

> At this point I feel compelled, as an Episcopal Layman, to express in writing my personal convictions of the proposed liturgical and Prayer Book changes presently being considered by the General Convention of the Episcopal Church.

> I strongly disagree with the proposed changes on the grounds that I dislike the idea of taking the 'Book of Common Prayer' and making of it a 'Common Prayer Book.'

In brief, rather than attempting to bring the word of God *down* to the level of mortal man, it is my contention that man, through the church, should be elevated to the high level of God.

For many hundreds of years the Bible has been studied throughout the world as it was originally written. Until comparatively recent years people have not felt it necessary to 'up-date' the word of God, or to simplify His word in order to make it more palatable or understandable.

Having read an article on Bishop Ivol Curtis of the Diocese of Olympia, Washington, in which the Bishop proclaimed that he strongly favored the proposed changes in liturgy of the Episcopal Church because he felt such changes would bring the church up-to-date and make the Bible more understandable, the author wrote Bishop Curtis, stating that he was sorry to have to disagree with the Bishop's stand on the liturgy changes and enclosed the foregoing, 'A Prayer For Our Beloved Church in Crisis'. The author asked Bishop Curtis' authorization to use the prayer in other parishes and missions within the Diocese of Olympia. However, the letter and request both went unanswered.

Dismayed at the continuing turn of events taking place within the Episcopal Church in June of 1977, Mr. Olzendam wrote the Presiding Bishop, John M. Allin proposing a national referendum as follows:

Proposing a Call by the Presiding Bishop for a National Open Clear Cut Referendum by the Individual Members of the Episcopal Church to Save the Episcopal Church In America.

Our Beloved Episcopal Church shudders in the winds of needless change.

Some 500,000 members have lately ceased to be members of our Episcopal Church.

Let us find out once and for all just what we, the members really think, not what our delegates to National Meetings think we think.

Our glorious Prayer Book of 400 years, second only to the Holy Bible in beauty of language and deep devotion, is carelessly altered.

Our Priesthood of a thousand years is tinkered with by delegates who seem to have forgotten how we the people feel about the Priesthood of Jesus Christ in 1977.

Our sense of decency has been shaken and defiled by some of the strange types of people being installed in the revered traditions of a church which, for lo, these many turbulent years, has been the bridge between Protestants and Roman Catholics.

Let us have a chance to vote to stop in its devastating tracks the splintering of our church into new churches and new Common Prayer Books.

Rise Up O Men and Women of God and speak out. Now is the time to make our voices heard in a great National Referendum of our members from Maine to California, from Florida to Washington and from Hawaii to Alaska.

Let us, the members, call on our Presiding Bishop to act now and lead us forward in the Power, Grace, Love and growth of Jesus Christ in the Episcopal Church in the United States of America in 1977-1978. Amen.

Copies of this referendum proposal were also mailed to the *New York Times, U.S. News and World Report, The Living Church* and *The Episcopalian*.

On July 9, 1977, the writer received the following reply to his letter from the Presiding Bishop Allin's assistant, The Reverend Richard J. Anderson:

Dear Mr. Olzendam:

Bishop Allin has asked me to thank you for your good letter of June 23 and for the proposal for a national referendum which you have suggested.

Bishop Allin appreciates your interest and your concern, and certainly shares your commitment to the Episcopal Church's future. He does not, however, feel that a national referendum would be practical or desirable. After giving the matter a great deal of thought, he has decided that what is really needed is more interest in the conventions and councils of our Church at all levels by the members of our Church. He is also conscious of the fact that the General Convention is an historic part of our heritage, and that its authority should not in any way be under-cut.

The Presiding Bishop is grateful to you, however, for having taken the time to present so thoughtful a proposal, and please know this letter comes with his thanks as well as with his best wishes.

Faithfully,

(The Rev.) Richard J. Anderson
Assistant to the
Presiding Bishop

Chapter Fourteen

Proposed Changes in "The Book of Common Prayer" Prove Controversial

In the July 10th (1977) issue of *The Living Church* Rod Olzendam came across an article titled *The Dignity of Choice* by The Reverend George W. Wickersham, II, rector of St. Luke's Church in Hot Springs, Virginia. The article, which also discusses the proposed liturgical changes in *The Book of Common Prayer*, so impressed Olzendam that he wrote for and received permission to reprint it.

> "The key to harmony
> turns on giving
> local churches

The Dignity of Choice
By George W. Wickersham, II

There was a resolution at our recent diocesan convention, a resolution addressed to the special commission set up by the last General Convention. The resolution asked that use of the 1928 *Book of Common Prayer* be permitted in our churches after 1979 (assuming that the Proposed Book will be authorized). There was discussion at the open hearings, but when the resolution, somewhat amended as a result of the hearings, came before the convention for a vote, it was tabled. Hence all debate on the matter was squelched. Thus our church deals with an item of grave concern to an enormous number of her people,

101

and thus she has been dealing, I might add, for the better part of a decade.

Oh yes, there have been questionnaires, committees ad nauseam, not to mention three different new books (or was it four?). The perfectly obvious fact remains that perhaps as many as half of our lay members are very unhappy with the results.

We are told that much of the old book is in the latest one, but the first thing which one notices is that much of it is not. Gone are the 'Great Bible' Psalms, the Epistles and Gospels (marvelous devotional material) and many of the most loved (and least loved) 'occasional offices' (even the marriage service!).

But this is not the point. The issue does not turn on the merits or demerits of the new book. It does not even turn on its acceptance or nonacceptance. I know very few Episcopalians who are not perfectly willing to see it authorized for use. The issue turns on the fact that there are literally millions who do not like it and far prefer the old book.

My parish serves a great resort hotel, famous also as a convention center. Our congregations usually include a number of its patrons. I have yet to meet a layman in the lot who likes the revisions. Where there is that kind of smoke, there must be considerable fire.

Introducing the revised book is not a matter of principle. Why have we forgotten this? We are not dealing with racial justice, opportunity for the poor or women's rights. We are simply dealing with the way we worship. The way that we have been worshiping is neither heretical nor in bad taste (to say the least!). It may be a little old-fashioned at points and in need of updating and supplementing. But what we have been given is a whole lot more than most of us ever bargained for. Absolutely nothing is to be gained by forcing it on us, except resentment.

Everywhere about us we hear voices crying 'Conciliation! Tolerance! Peacemaking!' These same voices should, therefore, encourage pursuit of the obvious course in this matter: the authorized use of both books. "No!" they cry. "We must have but one book and thus unify the church!" And thus divide it.

It has been my inestimable privilege to have had, during the past decade, two parishes in England (on an exchange basis). These two experiences have made American liturgical revision much harder for me to take. Revision in England has been carried on almost without incident, even though it is in many ways as radical as ours. For one thing the British never thought of bringing it out all at once—hundreds of pages of change, our own incredible method. No, one service at a time. But the main reason for the general acceptance of the new services lies in a short notice printed inside the cover of each one, stating categorically that it 'may not be used in. . .a parish without agreement of the Parochial Church Council.' (To us this would mean agreement on the part of the vestry.) And the 1662 book remains official and in all the churches.

The key to harmony in England, then, has turned on giving the local churches the dignity of choice. The people there are proud of what they do because *they* do it. Our attitude here, on the other hand, is essentially a medieval one. Goodness only knows why. We live in 'the land of the free,' but good old PECUSA acts as though her people were ignorant serfs who have to be told what to do. Actually, they are for the most part devout, educated people, albeit with a dreadful inferiority complex in the realm of religion. (And who is to blame for the latter?)

Now we further confound our troops by telling them that the book which we have held up to them as sacred for 300 years is no longer Kosher. How confusing can we get? No wonder many fear that we are changing the faith! (And they do.)

From a pastoral point of view, then, it appears to be of extreme importance that our bishops and other clerical and lay leaders begin right now to say that there is no need for this issue at all. Our preoccupation with an 'either-or' position is unwarranted. General Convention simply must accept the concept that the new book will have to win its own way at the local level.

If our leaders have the sagacity to do this, they will also be putting their weight behind the preservation in an official capacity of a book which is virtually unmatched for private devotions, the 1928 *Book of Common Prayer*.

As far as our pews are concerned, I have no doubt that the new book will ultimately prevail. If it has the qualities attributed to it by its proponents, certainly it will. But there is another factor which virtually assures its universal use. By and large, parishes seek to accomodate their clergy (for better or for worse). The clergy, ultimately, will all be trained in the new book and will, doubtless, want to use it.

None of this alarms me. I have worshiped with all sorts of books. The Lord has apparently listened anyway. A good enough liturgist could probably make the telephone book effective. What does alarm me is the great unhappiness over revision presently in our church. It is acute and it is widespread. Everywhere our lay people are shaking their heads. Malaise! And nothing could be more ineffective than a church without enthusiasm.

The fact remains that much of this discontent is completely unnecessary. Of course our people should have the option. Of course! And anyway why not? There is not a thing wrong with the old book. It has served us handsomely for many years. Is it suddenly sin? If we insist on discarding it in 1979 (or at some later date), we will only succeed in making untold numbers of our people unhappy, confused and angry. And the gain for our church? Zero.

Shortly after reading *The Dignity of Choice* Olzendam wrote Wickersham as follows:

Dear Wick:

I must congratulate you most heartily on your article 'Dignity of Choice'. I admire your capacity to use the English language in such a persuasive manner.

I am enclosing herewith a copy of a letter which I wrote to the Presiding Bishop together with his reply. . . .I called for a national referendum of the individuals in the Episcopal Church as to whether or not they want what goes on to continue. . . .

The Presiding Bishop's letter to me seems very sidetracked and no answer whatsoever to the problem. . . .Will we have to have a resolution asking for the use of the 1928 *Book of Common Prayer* in our churches after 1979? How shall we introduce such a resolution? For now is the time to begin this work if we are to have any influence on this situation which is being forced upon us.

Warmest regards,
Rod

In response to the Olzendam letter The Rev. Wickersham replied: (Excerpts from the letter follow).

My Dear Friend:

Your letter to the P.B. represents the anguished cry of (literally) millions of us. His answer is, I think, sympathetic and largely sincere. We cannot get around General Convention. It therefore falls upon us to introduce just such a resolution as you propose. To fascilitate this, General Convention set up a committee to study this matter. . . .

Hang in there, dear friend, we may find traces of the Divine Spirit in the old Church yet!   (Sincerely,) Wick

As has been pointed out in the foregoing writings, most Episcopalians do not want the proposed changes in *The Book of Common Prayer* forced upon them. For this, and other reasons it seems only fitting and proper that all members of the Episcopal Church, by referendum, have an opportunity to vote on this important issue when it comes before the General Convention in 1979. In the meantime, it behooves each and everyone of us to immediately express our likes or dislikes in writing relative to the proposed liturgical changes to the Presiding Bishop.

The Bowdlerization of
a Literary Treasure

Another Episcopalian who has made his views known through the printed media is John Omwake, editor of the Kingsport, Tennessee *Times-News Weekender*. Mr. Omwake's book review of *The Proposed Book of Common Prayer*, prepared by the Standing Liturgical Commission of the Episcopal Church and published by *Seabury Press* is reprinted here in its entirety:

Despite the title this very bulky (1,001 pages) book bears little resemblance to the genuine article. The genuine article is, of course, the historic *Book of Common Prayer* which has been used by the church of the Anglican Communion (including the Episcopal Church in this country) since 1549 when, in the midst of the Reformation the incumbent Archbishop of Canterbury, Thomas Cranmer, viewed the medieval Roman rites, separated the wheat from the chaff and translated that 'wheat' from the original Latin into a sonorous, majestic Tudor English which, to a large measure, has assured *The Book of Common Prayer* of a place along with The Authorized (King James) Version of the Bible and the works of William Shakespeare, among the treasures of the English language.

Despite a number of revisions (in 1552, 1558, 1662, 1789, 1892 and 1928) to meet the needs of a new day, the beauty and the genius of Cranmer's original have remained largely intact.

But no longer. The latest 'revision' authorized for use after the church's General Convention last year culminated more than 20 years of work by giving provisional approval (to be confirmed by a second vote in 1979 before the book becomes the official liturgy of the church), has turned nearly everything upside down.

Except in a few cases the beautiful Cranmerian language has been chucked out the window. Replacing it is a flat tasteless modern which often smacks of what one bishop of the church, disdainful of the new liturgy, has called a 'hey you, God, approach to deity'.

Thus in the marriage rite, the vows no longer read 'till death do us part' (one of the best-loved phrases in the book) but instead, 'until we are parted by death.' The giver of the ring no longer says, 'with this ring I thee wed' but rather the uninspired 'I give you this ring as a symbol of my vow.' The archaic (but easily understandable) 'thereto I give (plight) thee my troth' becomes simply, 'This is my solemn vow' (which as one observer has pointed out, is a disaster. How many times have we heard politicians uttering these same words with no intention of keeping them?)

The Proposed Book of Common Prayer abounds with such horrors. In Psalm 51, the well-known verse, 'Thou shalt purge me with hyssop, and I shall be clean; Thou shalt wash me and I shall be whiter than snow' has been laundered into 'Purge me from sin, and I shall be pure, wash me, and I shall be clean indeed'. Were the revisers afraid that the man (or woman) in the pew may not know what 'hyssop' is? Another example: 'Lord, now lettest thou thy servant depart in peace according to thy word' (Luke 2:29) now reads 'Lord, you have set your servant free to go in peace as you have promised.'

And in place of the rugged faith of the original, there is gross sentimentality. Take, for instance, a phrase from the 'Rite Two' order of the communion: 'He stretched out his arms upon the cross, and offered himself, in obediemce to your will, a perfect sacrifice for the whole world.' Not only is this corny and trite, it also reduces the Atonement to the level of the Oberammergau Passion Play. Christ becomes merely an actor on a stage.

The Standard Liturgical Commission, which drafted this mess, and many bishops and priests, who are assiduously working to see that the Proposed Book replaces the 1928 book (still the Episcopal Church's official book of worship) even before 1979, maintain that the new book preserves much of the historic *Book of Common Prayer*. In doing so, they point to the fact that the book provides forms of the communion service, morning and evening prayer and the burial office in the traditional Tudor English. True enough. The 'Rite One' communion service can be constructed in such a manner as to preserve the 1928 book's service fairly well intact. Morning and evening prayer present more of a problem, since one is constrained to use the SLC's translation of the Psalter, which is in flat, ugly modern English.

But everything else is in modern English: Baptism, confirmation, marriage, special services for Holy Week, ministry to the sick and the services for ordaining deacons, priests, and bishops. There is, I grant you, a rubric permitting these services to be conformed to traditional language when used in conjunction with a 'Rite One' service, but many bishops and priests probably are unaware of the rubric, much less would admit of its existence. (It's on Page 14.)

The Standing Liturgical Commission and its apologists among the clergy and laity maintain that the language must be modernized because the Tudor English of the old book is not easily understandable to the average worshiper. I contend this is a lot of hogwash, but the revisers desire to make the liturgy better understood would have been more admirable had they not played havoc with the historic faith of the church.

The whole thrust seems to be away from the spiritual toward the secular, toward the glorification of man at the expense of God. Penitence is reduced to an absolute minimum, a dangerous thing in a hedonistic age of little private preparation. The general confession and absolution may be omitted at any time, as may the Ten Commandments; the key phrases 'there is no health in us' (why else do we need the Lord?) and 'miserable offenders' (which we certainly are when we confess our sins) are gone from the general confession, and the book has been excised of most references to original sin and the devil. The revisers claim that this has been done to shift emphasis to the more positive, joyful act of thanksgiving in the eucharist, but I submit that it makes for a barren, meaningless act of worship if you can't make a good confession of your sins before entering into the thanksgiving portion of the service.

The baptismal rite has been similarly gutted. Any allusion in original sin is avoided. For example, the words said at the beginning of the signing of the cross in baptism, 'We receive this Child (Person) into the congregation of Christ's flock and do him (her) with the sign of the Cross, in token that hereafter he (she) shall not be ashamed to confess the faith of Christ crucified, and manfully to fight under the banner, against sin, the world, and the devil; and to continue Christ's faithful soldier and servant unto his (her) life's end' comes out in the wash as '(Name), you are sealed by the Holy Spirit in Baptism and marked as Christ's own for ever.' The result is both aesthetically and theologically deficient: The baptized person merely joins the ecclesiastical Club.

Last, but not least, a phrase in the modern English version of the Lord's Prayer warrants mention. 'And lead us not into temptation, but deliver us from evil' is translated as 'Save us from the time of trial, and deliver us from evil.' This is a very dangerous statement to make. After all, we do not ask to be saved from the time of trial; we are tempted daily. What we ask is that we be saved in the time of trial, in temptation. It is too bad that this deficiency was not corrected.

There is, to be sure, much that is good about the 'Proposed Book'. The additional congregational participation is to be welcomed, as well as the greater flexibility and a number of desired enrichments, many of which have been used unofficially for quite some time. The new table of lessons spread out over a three-year period, provides five times as much biblical material to be read during services, and the new calendar includes some well-deserved additions, such as Mary Magdalene. The ministry to the sick has been much improved in content (though not in language) and the burial office has been greatly enriched.

But all of this has been purchased at a terrible price. The historic *Book of Common Prayer* has been turned into a sort of liturgical 'I'm Okay, You're Okay'. One of the treasures of the English language has been bowdlerized. Let us hope that a future, wiser generation sees fit to rectify the errors of today's revisers and tinkerers.

—A review by John Omwake
Times-News Weekender Editor

Chapter Fifteen

A Miscellany of Christian Memorabilia

Roderic Marble Olzendam has long been a devout Episcopalian who, insofar as is humanly possible, practices daily, the tenets of his religion. At age 18, he was lay reader in New York City's Trinity School. To date, he has been a lay reader under five bishops in the Diocese of Olympia, Washington and has been authorized to preach his own sermons in the states of Washington and Arizona.

He has been privileged to have served as Senior Warden in three different Episcopal Churches and has served as Director of Public Relations for the Diocese of Olympia.

One of Rod's most memorable experiences occurred when Bishop Stephen Fielding Bayne, of the Diocese of Olympia, presented him with the 'Bishop's Cross' for his outstanding services to church and state. At the time, only one other person had ever received this distinguished citation.

The miscellaneous religious writings which follow are but a fraction of what he has written on this subject over the past 85 years.

A Baccalaureate Sermon

In 1968 Roderic Olzendam delivered the Baccalaureate Sermon before the graduating class of Orcas High School entitled 'Harken What the Lord God Will Say'. The text is from Psalm 80:19 and points up the importance of religion in our daily lives. The following is taken from that Sermon:

"Turn us again O Lord of Hosts, Show the light of thy countenance and we shall be whole'.

A Baccalaureate Sermon says Mr. Webster is one delivered to a graduating class at Commencement—a discourse delivered in public, usually by a clergyman for the purpose of religious instruction and grounded on a passage in Scripture.

Someone has truly said, "It is better to light one candle than to curse the darkness." So I am asking each one of you to light your own personal candle, and then to stride ahead, unafraid, confident and not 'cursing the darkness'.

"I am saying to you, look ahead with hope and with deep seated faith in the future, in spite of all national and international hubbub. And whatever you decide to do, or be, is your own personal decision. No one can decide for you.

"Almighty God in His infinite wisdom in creation gave to man a gift He gave to no other creature. The gift of choice. You are free to choose right and you are free to choose wrong.

"God defined 'right' and 'wrong'. If you don't know right from wrong, listen to your own conscience. Listen hard, for your guiding voice is planted by God deep in your very being.

"The Christian Church, founded by Jesus Christ in AD 33, is the most amazing institution on earth.

"The voice of Jesus Christ has had a more profound and lasting effect on the thinking of human beings than all the Kings, Emperors, Tzars, and Fuhrers and more than all the armies, navies and airforces combined.

"And yet, some fools proclaim 'God is dead'. In spite of man, the message of Christ still calls out strong and clear to those who listen.

"I am sure that you must feel the presence of God within this room tonight. I know I do.

"Please bear in mind that the men who have had the greatest effect on the founding and progress of this nation were God-fearing men who turned to God for help in times of crisis.

"Each of you is an individual, a distinct personality with a human soul to save, a part of God is within you.

"Are you ready, willing and eager to make your own contribution toward the preservation of all legitimate freedom?

"You will need the help of Almighty God, whose glory fills the universe.

"The Power of Almighty God is everywhere. Tune in on this wonderful station, station G-O-D. How? By sitting or kneeling and saying aloud or to yourself, 'God, I need your help'. Soon you will hear God speaking to you. Get the whole message and don't hang up before God has finished speaking.

"Don't feel frustrated if your prayer is not answered at once. Keep the line open. Then pray again tomorrow and all the tomorrows to come."

As a devout Episcopalian, Roderic Olzendam strongly disagrees with the proposed changes in 'The Book of Common Prayer' being considered by the General Convention on the grounds that 'I dislike taking 'The Book of Common Prayer' and making of it a 'common prayer book'.'

"Rather than attempt to bring the word of God down to the level of mortal man, it is my contention that man, through the church, should be elevated to the high level of God.

"For many hundreds of years the bible has been studied throughout the world as it was originally written. Until comparatively recent years people have not felt the necessity to update the word of God, or to simplify His word that it might be made more palatable, or understandable."

It was with this thought in mind that Olzendam wrote and delivered the following prayer in Emmanuel Church on Orcas Island in August of 1975:

A Prayer for our Beloved Church in Crisis

O Almighty God, who changeth not, Thou who art the First Great Cause of all living things, we come to Thee in deep humility, seeking Thy guidance.

Our Father in heaven, we see change in the affairs of men, and we need to know Thy will in all matters, but more especially do we pray for Thy guidance in the affairs of Thy Church.

We know it was Thou who wrote the changeless laws of nature which regulate the rising and the setting of the sun, the moon and the stars. We know the tides come and go, and the wind bloweth as it listeth, but always at Thy bidding. We know obedience to Thine immutable laws brings harmony to the universe.

O God, we yearn for harmony in the affairs of Thy Children.

As we continue to worship Thee, using our beloved Book of Common Prayer, is it Thy will that we should continue to express our awesome wonder at Thy magnificent creation; or is it Thy will that we change the quality of our petitions and become chatty in a new attempt at familiarity with Thee?

We pray to Thee to reveal to us Thy will in our manner of worshipping Thee. Grant that in our effort to make the prayer book significant to the common man that we do not make the Prayer Book itself, *common*.

We ask Thy help, O Heavenly Father, through Jesus Christ, our Blessed Lord and Savior.

—Amen

A Tribute to Father Glion Benson

In January of 1976, although my dear friend, Glion Benson* former Vicar of Orcas Island's Emmanuel Episcopal Church, is at this writing still living, albeit near death, I felt a strange compulsion to write the following tribute to this truly beautiful man:

> Farewell, our dear friend Glion,
> As the shadows lengthen and the evening comes
> And the busy world is hushed;

You are fast returning to eternity,
And we hate to see you go,
For our love for you is great!

Lo, these fifteen years have passed so quickly!
When first you came to Orcas
You were just beginning your ministry
Of loving service to your Blessed Lord
And the people of these San Juan Islands.

Your training and experience as a diesel engineer
Has stood you in good stead in your chosen field
Of human relations,
Human engineering, if you wish.
Two plus two equal four and not five
In civil engineering,
And you have proven the truth of this fact
In your great contribution to the relationships
Between human beings.
You have been so loyal, so devoted,
So generous, so kind, and so considerate.

And men and women, boys and girls, young and old,
Have come to you for counsel in ever greater numbers,
Going away with thankfulness and joy!

For you are your Lord's most joyous Lackey,
As you styled yourself;
Always happy, full of joy, you ministered to many,
Even to the closing days.

You piloted the Royal Cross, gift of the women
Of the Diocese,
From Island to Island, as you baptized our babies,
And later prepared them for confirmation
By Bishops Bayne, Lewis and Curtis; great men
Whom you honored in the faith.

You married our sons and our daughters,
And our grandsons and our granddaughters.
You touched their lives as you fished with them,
And trained them to serve
Almighty God at our altars in Emmanuel, Eastsound,
Grace on Lopez, and St. Thomas on Shaw.

You and your family and followers spent
Ten Thousand hours and more,
Building a lovely chapel on Lopez, called Grace.
And the people of Lopez named their meeting place
For you, 'Benson Hall', for they loved you.

And you led us in prayer in the little red
School House on Shaw Island.
And it was good.

In these latter days, your faithful followers
Gathered together,
To create a second 'Benson Hall'
At Eastsound,
For the expanding work of the mission,
Under the leadership of your able successor
Johnson West.

San Juan Mission grew in harmony and strength,
And generous have been the gifts to God's work
Under your leadership.

In all these good works you have been so ably
Aided, without stint, and loved beyond bounds,
By your blessed Jean, whom we call Mother Benson.
And your beautiful daughters Elspeth and Janet
With their five sons and daughters, your grandchildren.
Who adore you and Jean.
They, too, have loyally helped.

And when the time came for you to call it a day,
Bishop Curtis, recognizing your devotion
To your Lord and His Church,
Honored you with a worthy title,
'Canon Missioner of the Diocese of Olympia',
And lo, it was good.

Everyone knows of the comradeship between you
And the men who steer the Washington State fleet,
And those who open and close the gates or chains,
And clear the decks of the Chetzemoka,
And the Vashon, and later the Evergreen,
The Klickitat, the Nisqually, and the Kaleetan.
These rugged men hold you in high esteem.

And many ranchers acclaim you for your work.

The affection which the people of the Islands
Have for you is universal,
From the most distinguished
To the latest humble newcomer.

You have christened their yachts
And fished from their rowboats.

You have buried their wives
In the soil of Orcas,
And comforted these men in their sorrow.

And now comes your loyal successor, Johnson West,
To lead us in the enlarging work
Flowing from Benson Hall.

Farewell, Glion; Go hence in joy
To your waiting Lord.

Well done, good and faithful servant!
Enter into your well-earned rest.

We will never forget you!

(*On April 21, 1976, my good friend, Glion Benson passed
away.)

—Roderic Marble Olzendam

The Bishop and the Flea

Some years ago, while Director of Public Welfare for the State of Washington, Roderic Olzendam was asked to speak at the Episcopal diocesan convention in Seattle. To open his talk Olzendam told this delightful little story about a bishop and a flea which follows.

"Ladies and gentlemen I should like to begin my talk by telling you about the distinguished British flea who gathered his children around him one day and told them:

"My dear children, I am most anxious to tell you about myself as a young man. Now, you must remember that the consuming ambition of my life was to see a real, live Bishop close up. So when I heard that the Bishop of London was coming to our very own Cathedral on this particular day, I hopped on over to the church very early in the morning on the day he was to arrive. As a matter of fact, I was the very first one at church that day.

"Once inside, I hopped on down the long center aisle to what I thought would be an excellent vantage point on one of the end pews. And children, it was simply marvelous.

"The sun was streaming in through those glorious stained glass windows as the old verger came to open the massive cathedral doors. The organist began to play the great organ and the cathedral began to fill with people.

"Do you know, children, I could hardly contain myself, because I knew that at the very end of that lomg procession there would be a real, live bishop and I would see him close up.

"Presently I heard the joyous singing of the church choir and as I peered anxiously down the aisle I could see the crucifer and the choresters. And at the very end of the procession I could see the Bishop.

"I waited patiently, trying desperately to contain myself until the Bishop came alongside me. Presently, before I realized it I was looking directly into the Bishop's soulful blue eyes.

"Children, it was indeed a most auspicious moment, and one I had waited for all my life. Then, as the Bishop drew closer I noticed for the first time, his magnificent head of white, fluffy hair. And it was at this point that I could no longer control my emotions. I simply had to get even closer. So, with every ounce of strength I could muster, I leaped from the pew smack dab in the middle of the Bishop's back hair.

"And it was there, my dear children, that I met your darling mother."

Prayers for Every Occasion
To Help You in Your Daily Life

Over a period of 400 years these Prayers have been used in the Episcopal Book of Common Prayer. They have been used by many generations of worshippers with amazing results. Written by the finest minds in our Church, we include them for your devotions in the hope you too, will gain strength, comfort and confidence by their frequent use.

I.   *BIRTH*
     We yield thee hearty thanks, most merciful Father, that it hath pleased thee to regenerate this Child with thy Holy Spirit, to receive him for thine own Child, and to incorporate him into thy holy Church. And humbly we beseech thee to grant, that he, being dead unto sin, may live unto right-eousness, and being buried with Christ in his death, may also be partaker of his resurrection; so that finally, with the residue of thy holy Church, he may be an inheritor of thine everlasting Kingdom; through Christ our Lord. Amen.

II. *CONFIRMATION*
     Defend, O Lord, this thy Child with thy heavenly grace; that he may continue thine for ever; and daily increase in thy Holy Spirit more and more, until he come unto thy everlasting Kingdom. Amen.

III. *MARRIAGE*

O eternal God, Creator and Preserver of all mankind, Giver of all spiritual grace, the Author of everlasting life; Send thy blessing upon these thy servants, this man and this woman, whom we bless in thy Name; that they, living faithfully together, may surely perform and keep the vow and covenant betwixt them made, (whereof this Ring given and received is a token and pledge,) and may ever remain in perfect love and peace together, and live according to thy laws; through Jesus Christ our Lord. Amen.

IV. *ENCOURAGEMENT*

Almighty and everliving God, who makest us both to will and to do those things which are good, and acceptable unto thy Divine Majesty; We make our humble supplications unto thee for these thy servants, upon whom, after the example of thy holy Apostles, we have now laid our hands, to certify them, by this sign, of thy favour and gracious goodness towards them. Let thy fatherly hand, we beseech thee, ever be over them; let the Holy Spirit ever be with them; and so lead them in the knowledge and obedience of thy Word, that in the end they may obtain everlasting life; through our Lord Jesus Christ, who with thee and the same Holy Spirit liveth and reigneth ever, one God, world without end. Amen.

V. *PRAYER FOR OUR COUNTRY*

Almighty God, who hast given us this good land for our heritage; We humbly beseech thee that we may always prove ourselves a people mindful of thy favour and glad to do thy will. Bless our land with honourable industry, sound learning, and pure manners. Save us from violence, discord and confusion; from pride and arrogancy, and from every evil way. Defend our liberties, and fashion into one united people the multitudes brought hither out of many kindreds and tongues. Endue with the spirit of wisdom those to whom in thy Name we entrust the authority of government, that there may be justice and peace at home, and that, through obedience to thy law, we may show forth thy praise among the nations of the earth. In the time of prosperity, fill our hearts with thankfulness and in the day of trouble, suffer not our trust in thee to fail; all which we ask through Jesus Christ our Lord. Amen.

VI.   UNITY OF GOD'S PEOPLE
O God, the Father of our Lord Jesus Christ, our only Saviour, the Prince of Peace; Give us grace seriously to lay to heart the great dangers we are in by our unhappy divisions. Take away all hatred and prejudice, and whatsoever else may hinder us from godly union and concord; that as there is but one Body and one Spirit, and one hope of our calling, one Lord, one Faith, one Baptism, one God, and Father of us all, so we may be all of one heart and of one soul, united in one holy bond of truth and peace, of faith and charity, and may with one mind and one mouth glorify thee; through Jesus Christ our Lord. Amen.

VII.   MISSIONS
O God, who hast made of one blood all nations of men for to dwell on the face of the whole earth, and didst send thy blessed Son to preach peace to them that are far off and to them that are nigh; Grant that all men everywhere may seek after thee

and find thee. Bring the nations into thy fold, pour out thy Spirit upon all flesh, and hasten thy kingdom; through the same thy Son Jesus Christ our Lord. Amen.

VIII. FRUITFUL SEASONS
Almighty God, who hast blessed the earth that it should be fruitful and bring forth whatsoever is needful for the life of man, and hast commanded us to work with quietness, and eat our own bread; Bless the labours of the husbandman, and grant such seasonable weather that we may gather in the fruits of the earth, and ever rejoice in thy goodness, to the praise of thy holy Name; through Jesus Christ our Lord. Amen.

IX. RAIN
O God, heavenly Father, who by thy Son Jesus Christ hast promised to all those who seek thy kingdom, and the righteousness thereof, all things necessary to their bodily sustenance; Send us, we beseech thee, in this our necessity, such moderate rain and showers, that we may receive the fruits of the earth to our comfort and to thy honour; through Jesus Christ our Lord. Amen.

X. ARMED FORCES
O Lord God of Hosts, stretch forth, we pray thee, thine almighty arm to strengthen and protect the soldiers (servicemen) of our country. Support them in the day of battle, and in the time of peace keep them safe from all evil; endue them with courage and loyalty; and grant that in all things they may serve without reproach; through Jesus Christ our Lord. Amen.

XI.   NATIONAL LEADERS AND HEROES

Almighty God, our heavenly Father, in whose hands are the living and the dead; We give thee thanks for all those thy servants who have laid down their lives in the service of their country. Grant to them thy mercy and the light of thy presence, that the good work which thou hast begun in them may be perfected; through Jesus Christ thy Son our Lord. Amen.

XII.   SCHOOLS

O Lord Jesus Christ, who dost embrace children with the arms of thy mercy, and dost make them living members of thy Church; Give them grace, we pray thee, to stand fast in thy faith, to obey thy word, and to abide in thy love; that, being made strong by the Holy Spirit, they may resist temptation and overcome evil, and may rejoice in the life that now is, and dwell with thee in the life that is to come; through thy merits, O merciful Saviour, who with the Father and the Holy Ghost livest and reignest one God, world without end. Amen.

XIII.   PERSONS GOING TO SEA

O Eternal God, who alone spreadest out the heavens, and rulest the raging of the sea; We commend to thy almighty protection, thy servant, for whose preservation on the great deep our prayers are desired. Guard him, we beseech thee, from the dangers of the sea, from sickness, from the violence of enemies, and from every evil to which he may be exposed. Conduct him in safety to the haven where he would be, with a grateful sense of thy mercies; through Jesus Christ our Lord. Amen.

XIV. **GOOD WORKS**
Direct us, O Lord, in all our doings, with thy most gracious favour, and further us with thy continual help; that in all our works begun, continued and ended in thee, we may glorify thy Holy Name, and finally, by thy mercy, obtain everlasting life; through Jesus Christ our Lord. Amen.

XV. **DEATH**
O God, whose mercies cannot be numbered; Accept our prayers on behalf of the soul of thy servant departed, and grant him an entrance into the land of light and joy, in the fellowship of thy saints; through Jesus Christ our Lord. Amen.

XVI. **FOR QUIET CONFIDENCE**
O God of Peace, who has taught us that in returning and rest we shall be saved, in quietness and in confidence shall be our strength; By the might of thy Spirit lift us, we pray thee, to thy presence, where we may be still and know that thou art God; through Jesus Christ our Lord. Amen.

Emmanuel Episcopal Church, Eastsound Village, Orcas Island, as it appears from the water.

A 17th Century Nun's Prayer

LORD, Thou knowest better than I myself know that I am
growing older and will some day be old.
Keep me from the fatal habit of thinking I must say something
on every subject and on every occasion.
Release me from craving to straighten out everybody's affairs.
With my great store of wisdom, it seems a pity not to use it all,
but Thou knowest, Lord, that I want a few friends at the end.
Keep my mind free from the recital of endless details; give me
wings to get to the point.
Seal my lips on my aches and pains. They are increasing and
love of rehearsing them becomes sweeter as the years go by.
I dare not ask for grace enough to enjoy the tales of others' pains,
but help me to endure them with patience.
I dare not ask for improved memory, but for growing humility
and a lessening cocksureness when my memory clashes with
the memories of others.
Teach me the noble lesson that, occasionally, I may be mistaken.
Keep me reasonably sweet; I do not want to be a Saint—some
of them are so hard to live with; but a sour old person is one
of the crowning works of the Devil.
Give me the ability to see good things in unexpected places and
talents in unexpected people. And give me, O Lord, the grace
to tell them so.

Bishops Who Have Served Emmanuel Church

The Rt. Rev. John Adams Paddock, 1880-1894.

The Rt. Rev. William Morris Baker (Interim Administrator), 1894-1901.

The Rt. Rev. Frederick William Keator, 1902-1924.

The Rt. Rev. Simeon Arthur Huston, 1925-1947 (Resigned).

The Rt. Rev. Stephen Fielding Bayne, Jr., 1947-1959. The first Angelican Executive officer under Archbishop of Canterbury in 1959.

The Rt. Rev. William Fisher Lewis, 1960, died in September of 1964.

The Rt. Rev. Ivol Ira Curtis, 1964-1976.

The Rt. Rev. Robert E. Cochrane, 1976-

Contributions and Memorials
Emmanuel Church, Orcas Island

Over the years residents of Orcas Island have lavished a great deal of spiritual love on Emmanuel Church. This love has shown itself in numerous ways. For example, countless hours of volunteer work by parishoners and St. Agnes Guild members, individually and collectively, have gone into the maintenance of this church. Parishoners have also added to the warmth and charm of Emmanuel Church through their generous contributions of such items as pews, stained glass windows, prayer and hymnal books, carpeting, bell and tower, to name but a few.

A partial list of those in whose names commemorative gifts have been made to the church over the years include: Altar boy, John Michael O'Dell 1942-1968 killed in the Viet Nam War, Saint Michael window to the west of the narthex was given in his memory; the Saint Luke window to the east of the narthex was given in 'Memory of Lloyd Palmer Sterns 1946-1967' who was killed in the Viet Nam War; the Agnus Di (Lamb of God) rose window at the end of the nave which is surrounded by symbols of the four Evangelists, Matthew, Mark, Luke and John, was given in memory of Howard H. Wright. Benjamin Franklin Avary is honored by American and Church flags which were given by Roderic Olzendam in loving memory of his best friend. A stained glass window to the right of the altar is in memory of John William Dickson 'Beloved priest and pastor from 1895-1904'.

A recent (1978) photograph of Emmanuel Church. The bell and belfry were added in 1967. *(Photo by Gordon Keith)*

The southwest window in the sanctuary is in memory of Sidney R.S. Gray, priest, founder and builder of Eastsound Episcopal Church from 1885-1893, (1853-1940). Inscribed on a wall plaque in back of the piano are the words: "In loving memory of Charles W. Shattuck who donated this church site in 1886." A third plaque reads: 'In loving memory of Emilie Harding Gow, member 1896-1904.'

The rose window (All Saint's Window) at the south end of the sanctuary is in memory of George Herbert Williams 1853-1935; the east and west choir windows were presented to the church in 1941 by Robert Moran. The crucifix which hangs over the Chancel Crossing and the Processional Cross which stands to the west of the altar were given in memory of Philip Tvete, 1953.

On the east wall, opposite the first three rows of pews, are four plaques which read as follows: 'In loving memory of Mary Waldrip Benson 1872-1922;' 'In loving memory of Harding Murdock Gow 1872-1947' and 'In loving memory of Alice G. Geoghegan 1875-1942'.

The seven hanging lamps over the altar symbolizing the seven gifts of the Holy Spirit were brought around the Horn as were the four hanging lamps in the nave. The three-branch candlesticks are in memory of Roy De Witt Burghardt. Another three-branch candlestick is in memory of May Burghardt. The altar is a memorial to Sidney Head while the altar rail and bishop's chair dated 1670 came from a bombed out church in England during the second World War and were presented to the church by Mr. and Mrs. Louis Brechemin of Deer Harbor.

The crystal cruets were given by Genevieve Wright, the Eucharistic candlesticks are in memory of Dr. Carl Moran's mother and the offering plates are in memory of Philip Tvete.

The church's first bell and tower were presented to Emmanuel Church during a special dedication sermon which was preached by Roderic Olzendam during the summer of 1967. The dedication plaque reads: "This bell and tower are placed here to the Glory of Almighty God, by Roderic Marble Olzendam, Sarah Dorothy Olzendam, 1967.'

Roderic Olzendam rings Emmanuel Church's bell to announce the opening of St. Agnes Guild's Annual Sale (1977). The clarion call of the bell evidently proved a bit too much for this lady's eardrums. *(Photo by Gordon Keith)*

On May 17, 1977 during the regular church service a new altar was dedicated 'To the Glory of God' in memory of Sidney R. Head. Sidney was born May 15, 1891 in Victoria, B.C., the son of Frederick George and Beatrice Gordon Head, two of the original members of Emmanuel Church. He was baptized on July 5th, 1891 at the age of seven weeks. His mortal remains were buried from Emmanuel Episcopal Church, April 18th, 1971.

Index

About the Authors

Roderic Olzendam
P.O. Box 195
Freedom Point
Orcas Island, WA. 98280

Roderic Marble Olzendam has been an active layman in the
Episcopal Church throughout most of his life. At age eighteen
he was lay reader on New York's Trinity School. Since then he
has been a lay reader under five Bishops in the Diocese of
Olympia, Washington and is authorized to preach his own
sermons in the States of Washington and Arizona. Mr.
Olzendam has also served as Senior Warden in four churches
and was Director of Public Relations for the Diocese of
Olympia. For his outstanding services to Church and State he
received the Bishop's Cross from the Diocese of Olympia in
Washington State.

During his distinguished career in the field of Industrial and
Public Relations, Mr. Olzendam held positions with the Spanish
River Pulp & Paper Mills Ltd. of Canada, Metropolitan Life In-
surance Company, Weyerhaeuser and *Reader's Digest*. He was
also Industrial Relations Advisor at the International Labor
Office at the League of Nations in Geneva, Switzerland, and

later became Director of Public Welfare for the State of Washington.

Although Mr. Olzendam lives in 'retirement' on Orcas Island in the State of Washington's San Juan Archipelago, he is still very active in the Episcopal Church. Over the years Mr. Olzendam has been the recipient of three 'Freedom Foundations Awards' for his patriotic writings. One of his recent retirement projects was the publication of his autobiography *Liberty's Grandson*.

Gordon Keith
P.O. Box 280
Eastsound, Wa. 98245

Gordon Keith, former Publisher/Editor of the national magazine *Dance Digest* is currently a feature writer for the *Islands' Sounder*, a bi-monthly newspaper published in the San Juan Islands. His articles and feature stories have been published in a variety of newspapers and magazines throughout the country. Keith's book *The James Francis Tulloch Diary 1875-1910* which he compiled and edited was published in 1978. Currently he is hard at work on a book about his favorite subjects: the San Juan Islands and those who inhabit them, titled *Voices From the San Juan Islands*.